# The Spiritual Autopsy of a Backslider

Janay Roberson

Copyright © 2019 Janay Roberson

All rights reserved. No portion of this book may be reproduced in any form without permission from the publisher, except as permitted by U.S. copyright law. The use of short quotations or occasional page copying for personal or group study is permitted and encouraged.

Unless otherwise noted, all Scripture is taken from the HOLY BIBLE, NEW INTERNATIONAL VERSION®, NIV®
Copyright © 1973, 1978, 1984, 2011 by Biblica, Inc.® Used by permission. All rights reserved worldwide.

Scriptures marked NLT are taken from the HOLY BIBLE, NEW LIVING TRANSLATION (NLT): Scriptures taken from the HOLY BIBLE, NEW LIVING TRANSLATION, Copyright©
1996, 2004, 2007 by Tyndale House Foundation. Used by permission of Tyndale House Publishers, Inc., Carol Stream, Illinois 60188. All rights reserved. Used by permission.

Scripture quotations marked "MSG" are taken from *THE MESSAGE*, copyright © 1993, 2002, 2018 by Eugene H. Peterson. Used by permission of NavPress. All rights reserved. Represented by Tyndale House Publishers, Inc.

Printed in the United States of America ISBN 978-0-57853-241-7
Published by: Awaken U Publishing Company
www.janayroberson.com

# Table of Contents

Introduction ................................................................. 1

1. The Walking Dead ................................................ 7

2. Identity Crisis ...................................................... 21

3. Internal Examination ......................................... 41

4. Mind Control ...................................................... 63

5. The Struggle Is Real .......................................... 87

6. Faith on Trial ..................................................... 129

7. Pray It Through ................................................. 161

8. Allow Me to Reintroduce Myself .................... 181

# Introduction

Let's take a trip down memory lane. Get that moment in your mind – you know – that moment, the day you decided to completely surrender to God. It was an amazing feeling, right? You felt as if a ton of bricks had been lifted off your shoulders.

You told yourself, your pastor, friends, and probably even those on Facebook you were making a change for the better. You were getting rid of the unnecessary baggage and people who would hinder you from going deeper into God. Out with the old and in with the new!

Your mindset shifted, and you were determined to get everything God had for you. You were on fire for the Lord. You got up early in the morning to spend quality time with Him by reading the Bible, and you even developed a prayer life. You posted scriptures and inspirational messages on social media. I mean, they couldn't tell you "nothing"!

Your walk was different. Your talk was different. Others could tell a certain change was taking place in your life. You were on a spiritual high, so you even started being nice to that rude co-worker who got on your last nerve.

And then... life happened. You became a student, a parent, got married, separated or divorced. Perhaps you got a job or lost one. Maybe you bought a house and relocated or the bank foreclosed on your property because of hard times. Whatever the case, you found yourself slowly drifting away from God. Either the pleasures or cares of life changed your outlook and priorities. You lacked the momentum you had to seek God wholeheartedly. Hence, the 30 minutes you once spent with Him diminished to 20 minutes, and before you knew it – it was almost nonexistent.

You found it hard to even open your mouth to say, "Thank you, Lord, for another day!" Although you had a Bible app on your phone, you didn't even have enough strength to read one scripture a day. And the Lord forbid if someone tried to come to you for encouragement. Honey, you would duck and dodge so fast because honestly, you were too empty on the inside to pour anything into anyone else.

Sound familiar? Yep, I know because just like you, I was in that same place. Many times, it was as if I was on a rollercoaster ride with its loops, climbs, and dives. Contemporary R&B singer Vivian Green may have called it an "Emotional Rollercoaster," but mine was spiritual.

Some seasons in my life went well. Of course, life wasn't perfect, but I had mastered the art of balancing my spiritual life in the midst of chaos. I would journal to God, have scheduled Monday date nights with Him and send encouraging text messages to people. It felt amazing to pour into the lives of others. But somewhere along the line, God got put on the back burner of my life. He was no longer immediately important. I was so busy with my job, new boo, friends, school, aspirations, and all the other things I decided to make a priority over Him. Before I knew it, my life was like a whirlwind, and I had nothing left in my spiritual reservoir to sustain me.

I had no fellowship with God. Attending church was less of a priority, and reading the Bible was far from my mind. In fact, life seemed very unfair, and my unbelief grew stronger, while my faith got weaker. Consequentially, the door for me to revert to my old ways opened wide and slowly but surely, I drifted into a backslidden state.

What does it mean to backslide? It is a Christian relapsing to old habits or bad ways after having a close relationship with God. How does a Christian get to that state? It generally comes with continued seasons of disobedience, rebellion, and sinful behaviors without repentance. However, there is actually another dimension of backsliding. It is not only the act of going back into sin, but it can also be the failure to go forward spiritually. At its core, backsliding is turning away from God, our faith, being complacent about spirituality, and ultimately, neglecting our commitment to Christ.

The enemy's lies wax stronger as our belief and trust in God deplete. Shortly, disappointment, fear, shame, and guilt consume every thought. You become so entangled, there seems to be no relief, hope, restoration or way of escape. Is there a way back to spiritual health? Can you break free from your backslidden condition?

The purpose of this book is to bring awareness to the backslidden state an increasing number of believers find themselves in. At the same time, it will identify the signs, symptoms, and habits of persons who have backslidden, those who are slowly drifting away from God and the ones seeking to help others who have lost their way. Moreover, as you read, you will find solutions to help you rise from the pit of unbelief, uncertainty, and apostasy.

God was specific when He spoke to me about those who are far away from Him, those sinking deep in sin but ready to be resurrected to their first love. He was detailed in regards to those who are ready to give this "God thing" one more try and loosen the grip of sin on their lives.

As you read, I pray the Holy Spirit will minister to you in a way that captivates your heart. May you identify why you became spiritually depleted. You will be equipped with powerful tools to build the hope, faith, and strength you need to get up and fight for your faith, and strength you need to get up and fight for your faith, as well as your future. Let the fire for God be rekindled in your life! I declare and decree, this time,

Introduction

the fire will never burn out again!

# Chapter 1
# The Walking Dead

> As for you, you were dead in your transgressions and sins, in which you used to live when you followed the ways of the world and of the ruler of the kingdom of the air, the spirit who is now at work in those who are disobedient. All of us also lived among them at one time, gratifying the craving of our flesh and following its desires and thoughts. Like the rest, we were by nature deserving of wrath (Ephesians 2:1-3).

For as long as I can remember, I have always loved criminal investigation shows. *Law & Order: Criminal Intent, Law & Order: Special Victims Unit (SVU)* and *The First 48* are three of my personal favorites. The purpose of these three shows is one and the same: to solve a crime. Whether it's murder, assault, abuse or rape, the detectives are determined to crack the case. They will do whatever is necessary to solve the crime and bring peace or closure to victims and their families.

Now, let's be honest. We all have a movie we watch over and over wishing the end would be different each time we watch it. No matter how much I watch *The First 48,* I always hope the victim survives his or her injuries. Unfortunately, 99% of the time the person ends up dying on the scene or later at the hospital.

*Law & Order* always has some sort of uncertainty attached to each episode, which makes it harder for me to determine the outcome of the case. I am excited when the victim survives the attack because it gives a different twist to the plot, adds to the suspense and helps the detectives solve their open case.

I love happy endings, but there are times on *Law & Order* and in real life when the victims die due to the severity of their injuries. Depending on the case, the detectives may request an autopsy from the coroner.

## What is an Autopsy?

*Merriam-Webster Dictionary* defines an autopsy as "an examination of a body after death to determine the cause of death or the extent of changes produced by disease – called also *necropsy*."

Autopsies are usually done for forensic purposes when suspicious circumstances surround someone's death or when no signs of natural causes can be located. They can also be performed for disease research, medical training or other educational purposes. But the ultimate reason is to discover the reason why death occurred.

The popular TV shows we love don't show us the

full process of getting an autopsy. Of course, television is all about the hype and suspense but in reality, several steps are taken before the autopsy is performed.

1. Investigators gather all the information about the subject and detail the events leading to the victim's demise

2. A careful inspection of the body is done to establish the victim's identity: weight, height, eye color and for clues to the cause of death

3. An internal examination is done starting with a "Y-shaped incision" of the chest. The pathologist removes the chest, abdominal, and pelvic organs to dissect them. If necessary, they will remove the brain to do further investigation.

4. Following the examination, the organs will either be returned to the body or cremated, depending on the family's wishes.

As you can see, an autopsy requires a detailed examination to determine the cause of a victim's death.

How does this relate to believers? If we take the time out of our busy schedules to peruse the church as a whole, we will find behind the church facades, many Christians are spiritual victims in need of spiritual autopsies. They need internal examinations that reach the recesses of their minds, souls, and hearts. It will reveal the root of the problems so they can be effectively dealt with. The reality is sexual immortality, depression, rejection, bitterness, and addiction – just to name a few, are slowly disconnecting people from God.

Unfortunately, many of us would reject the idea that we need an autopsy because we have become comfortable living in dysfunction. Religion has painted a false, dangerous portrait in the minds of believers that as long as others don't know about their mess, then it is cool. Hence, it has become the popular "trend" for pastors to sleep around with members. Women sell their bodies just to get enough cash to feed their children, others battle the thoughts of suicide, and men and women walk around with love for the opposite sex that they can't seem to shake.

Despite the public display of a happy life, the sad reality is that many people are living in private despair. They desperately want freedom from their jacked-up lifestyles. However, the drought of mercy and grace in a place that is supposed to be a house of the liberator – the church – has become a hindrance.

Instead of helping our brothers and sisters, we judge them harshly and condemn them to our own personal hell. However as Christians, it is not our job to judge and condemn people to hell, but it is our job to help reconcile them with the Father and provide a safe place for them to heal and recover.

Over the years, our churches have become gathering places for the "perfect." Many have failed to realize that the moment any of our messed up selves enter, it immediately becomes imperfect. In fact, in Mark 2:17, Jesus said those who are healthy do not need a doctor but those who are sick. This was His response to the Pharisees who accused Him of eating with sinners and tax collectors. His fundamental principle was that He didn't come to the world to help those who called themselves righteous but the ones who knew they were sinners in need of God's grace and mercy.

That is good news for you and me. No matter what failures, weaknesses or sins you associate yourself with, Jesus, the Great Physician, is ready and able to heal, deliver, and set free. Expect your mind to recall the bad things you have done. The enemy will bombard you with lies that your sins are too big and too many for Jesus to forgive. However, the Bible tells us in 1 John 1:9 that if we confess our sins, God is faithful and just to forgive us our sins and purify us from all unrighteousness.

"All" includes that blunt you rolled, that married man you slept with, that pornography you watched, those thoughts you had, that time you cussed out your boss, and even when you got pregnant out of wedlock!

Yes! All of that can be forgiven according to 1 John 1:9.

I would dare to say if an autopsy was performed on many believers to examine their spiritual states, the results would be quite shocking. Truth be told, no matter how beautiful the tongues, how fancy the hat or even how long the dress, it doesn't exempt any of us from backsliding. We are all prone to quickly slip into a spiritually depleted place. The reality is that behind social media posts and Sunday best selfies, many Christians aren't living; they are merely existing. They are literally "The Walking Dead."

The time comes in our lives when we are depleted physically, mentally, emotionally, and unfortunately, spiritually. For various reasons, we lose hope and faith. Our spiritual lives just don't seem worth it. We are spiritually dead. It's a dangerous yet common state to be in and if not careful, it will lead to backsliding. We revert to our old habits and sinful nature. Our hearts turn far away from God and we engage in activities that displease Him without any regard for His commandments.

> But they refused to pay attention; stubbornly they turned their backs and covered their ears. (Zechariah 7:11)

Backsliding is not a new phenomenon for the church. In the Bible, we read several accounts of backsliders. The prophet Jeremiah addressed the Israelites on multiple occasions about true repentance and returning to God. The prophet Hosea describes God's love toward a people who are wayward and have no regard for God or His ways.

To paint a vivid picture of the dilemma of those who backslide, Scripture describes them as dogs returning to their vomit (Proverbs 26:11, 2 Peter 2:18).

Gross, right? But that is exactly what many are doing – returning to the things that caused the most pain, stress, misery, and heartache.

When many people come to know Jesus Christ as their personal Savior, they have good intentions. They genuinely desire to surrender to Him and give up everything that breaks His heart. They stop going to certain places, hanging out with certain people, and doing certain things. Of course, some people keep a slight grip on the past, but others actually release their grip for this new walk.

As life goes on, there are times we come face-to-face with the things we once left. The temptation is strong, and we are overtaken by uncertainty. Unfortunately, we take that first step into the abyss of sin and that step leads to another and another until we become relaxed thinking we are safe and our actions are justified.

That's how backsliding slowly creeps into the life of a Christian. It is a gradual process that can start with a single thought, disappointment or giving in to our fleshly desires.

Backsliding wouldn't be a problem if it happened all at once because we could identify it and handle it properly. However, the enemy is deceptive and has to stick to his sneaky tactics. He will use the things he knows will catch our attention, divert our thoughts and lead us in the wrong direction. And he does it in our most vulnerable seasons. Consequently, our fellowship with God is broken.

Don't make the mistake of thinking you are so "deep" and righteous you will never fall victim to Satan's tactics. If you do, you are the perfect target for the devil. 1 Corinthians 10:12 warns us, "So if you think you are standing firm, be careful that you don't fall" (NIV).

Knowing a few scriptures won't keep you from backsliding. Satan is well-versed in Scripture – probably better than some of us. Therefore, if we are not careful, we will be quickly knocked off our high horses and made to face the harsh reality of backsliding.

**Symptoms of Backsliding**

Diagnosing when we are backsliding can be hard because we don't like unearthing and confronting our dark side. For some, it's too painful, while others don't want to believe they would even contemplate turning away from God. It is also because we are experts at pinpointing other people's faults but the irony is we don't ever see what is wrong with us.

Let me help you! Deliverance is not in the cover-up but in the conviction, which leads to confession. We are more effective when we confront our realities, not deny them.

There are certain seasons in your life when you are most prone to backsliding. These include:

1. When you are habitually sexually active

without conviction

2. When you stop reading the Word and fellowshipping with God

3. When prayer is no longer a necessity but the last resort

4. When you stop attending church or have no desire to find a good church home

5. When every comment others make about your spiritual state offends you

6. When you entertain thoughts and engage in activities you previously let go

7. When you hang out with people you vowed to stop socializing with once you accepted Christ into your life

8. When you feel as if you have no purpose or identity in the world

9. When you fit in with the world more than you do the church

10. When holiness is no longer your goal

11. When worship is no longer a vital part of your daily life.

12. When you come into agreement with the enemy's lies

If you identify with any of these symptoms, chances are you have backslidden and your heart is far away from God. You have stopped abiding in God and have allowed the old man to arise and suffocate the new you. When you find comfort in this state, it will ultimately lead to your downfall. Getting out of this poor spiritual condition requires that you get up, face whatever has a hold on you and fight for your freedom as a child of God.

I know it is easier said than done, but the amazing thing about our God is His unconditional love. Even when we fall, He is there like a loving and concerned parent ready to give us a hand back up.

The Prodigal Son left home to do his own thing, but he quickly found out that his way was definitely not the best way. He returned home just for his father to throw him a party on his arrival. Although the elder son remained faithful to his father and never left home, that didn't hinder the father from equally loving the one who departed. That's the way our heavenly Father operates. He waits patiently to show compassion to His sons and daughters.

> What do you think? If a man owns a hundred sheep, and one of them wanders away, will he not leave the ninety-nine on the hills and go to look for the one that wandered off? And if he finds it, truly I tell you, he is happier about that one sheep than about the ninety-nine that did not wander off (Matthew 18:12-13).

This scripture shows God loves you so much He would leave the ninety-nine just to rescue you! How amazing and mind-blowing is that?! That is how much He loves and adores you! God is married to the backslider and it is His goodness which leads us to repentance.

> Turn, O backsliding children, saith, the Lord; for I am married unto you: and I will take you one of a city, and two of a family, and I will bring you to Zion. (Jeremiah 3:14 KJV)

No matter what the enemy tries to make you believe, please know that you are needed here on this earth. You have the right to be revived, refreshed, and restored. How do you begin to write that new chapter in your life? It simply starts with you making a decision to experience the abundant life Jesus promised you. Even in the midst of what seems like the hardest thing yet, remember there is no complication too deep or sin so great that can prevent God from restoring you if you choose to follow the process.

The Spiritual Autopsy of a Backslider

## **Spiritual Assessment**

Take a moment to reflect on your current spiritual state. Have you stopped spending time with God, other believers or attending church?

_____
_____
_____

What is blocking your connection to the Father?

_____
_____
_____

What hinders your spiritual walk?

_____
_____
_____
_____

Now that you have that in mind, write down and elaborate on your answers in a notebook or in your journal, so you can see them. Let God speak to you, so you can take the steps to become the person He has called you to be – spiritually whole.

# Chapter 2
# Identity Crisis

> Before I formed you in the womb I knew you, before you were born I set you apart; I appointed you as a prophet to the nations (Jeremiah 1:5 NIV).

One afternoon during my undergraduate years, I had finished my classes for the day and decided I would go to my dorm to take a quick nap before heading to the library. As I drifted into what I thought was a light sleep, I began to dream. It was no ordinary dream. Actually, it was quite eye-opening and jaw-dropping.

In this dream, there were two persons: a woman and me. What was interesting about this dream was I could see the woman, but she couldn't see me.

As I watched her, I had several reactions to what I was witnessing. I saw compromise and depression unveiling itself, and a life that was slowly slipping away from the very foundation her life was built on as a child. I shook my head in dismay, gasped, and even yelled at her, but she never saw or heard me.

The dream continued, and I was forced to see further into her world. I recall seeing her smile, laugh, cry, and frown within moments. Her life seemed normal, and she appeared to be living her best life. At least, that's what I thought.

While observing so much within a few moments, I noticed her emotions were far from stable. It was sad to watch. From the outside looking in, she looked like the perfect college sophomore. However, on the inside, she was miserable, insecure, and lost. She was completely helpless, but I couldn't do anything to help her. That wasn't the saddest part. The most despondent aspect of that dream was "she" was actually me. Yep! That emotionally unstable girl I was looking at in the dream was me. Crazy, isn't it? I thought the same thing.

My future self was looking back at the present me. This dream gave me the opportunity to take a deeper look at myself. I got the chance to see who I really was. I admit. It didn't feel too great. It was as if I was standing in front of a mirror looking at myself. But the revelation was far more than what the natural eye could comprehend. I was shocked!

My self-worth was based on man's opinion of me. I tried to fit in with different groups, social organizations and worked multiple jobs to gain a sense of security. Looking back, I missed out on precious moments because of my underlying fears, doubts, and lack of trust in God. I hadn't found myself yet, so I tried to walk in someone else's shoes. I tried to meet the unrealistic expectations others placed on me, not realizing I was dealing with an identity crisis. Yikes! Identity crisis? Sounds very harsh, doesn't it?

Well, if you are anything like that girl in the dream not knowing who you are, your worth, and value, eventually, you too will find yourself with an identity crisis.

**Identity Matters**

Before an autopsy can be performed, the coroner has to make a positive identification of the deceased's body. This can be done in several ways. One of the first things a coroner does on the victim is document the clothing worn at the time of death. This can go a long way, especially in a case where someone is missing.

Checking clothing, jewelry, and shoes is a significant part of the process since they can be exclusive to certain people. The coroner will even go further to record any tattoos, piercings or other unique marks that may be on the individual.

Families usually appreciate this strenuous process as it helps with the accurate identification of the deceased. In years past, families were called in to identify the body of their loved one but later found out it was a case of mistaken identity.

Similarly, many Christians have mistaken their identities and conformed to who the world thinks they should be. Hence, they live below their full potential or in a lane they were never called to. Consequently, their identities are at risk of being tainted and manipulated by man's expectations and opinions of them. If you are like that, you will not only see your identity and purpose through the lens of your past failures and shortcomings, you will also operate as such. Dwelling on your past can lead to backsliding because it prevents you from moving forward. It stops you from being the man and woman God created you to be and pushes you outside of His will for your life.

As children, we had countless dreams, visions, and desires. We would dress up as our favorite characters, celebrities or idols. We believed we could do anything. As we grew, we had plans to make something out of our lives and emulated those who succeeded because we wanted to achieve as well. However, while it is perfectly normal to have heroes and those we look up to, the problems come when we idolize them. Our obsession with these people causes us to neglect the beauty, uniqueness, and greatness God imparted into us as individuals.

"Comparison is the death of joy" (Mark Twain). When we compare ourselves to others and make plans for our lives based on their lifestyles, unhappiness prevails. We feel like failures when we don't measure up. And I get it! We all want to be secure and have a wonderful future. We want to graduate from college or accomplish certain goals before hitting the big 30. We have vision board parties and expect our dreams to manifest. But sometimes, it just doesn't happen. If we are honest, many of us will admit we are still trying to figure out who we are, what our purpose on earth is and what the future looks like. Purpose is significant to our growth and success. It gives meaning to life, as well as a sense of worth and value. Our purpose makes us push and go on just a little more, even when we don't feel like it.

The right perspective on the journey to purpose is a must. The moment you take matters out of your own hands and hand them over to God, your perspective will completely shift. The most humbling experience is when God literally squashes every plan you thought you had in order for His plan to manifest in your life.

> Many are the plans in a person's hear, but it is the Lord's purpose that prevails. (Proverbs 19:21)

I used to say, "Here, God! Here are my plans. They look amazing, right? Even though I created them based off of my preferences and out of frustration, I still think they are good. So God, do what you do best with them."

I'm sure God was looking at me like, "Girl...you tried it! But you must have forgotten that I knew you before you were even in your mother's womb. Trust that I know the plans I have for you; they are to prosper and not harm you. They are plans to give you hope and a future."

God had holy plans for us even before we saw the light of the day! Which means He knows what is best for us and we can't continue to make it as though God is obligated to do or bless anything that is out of His will. Regardless of our impatience or feelings.

For some reason, we think our plans are better than His in every area: career, relationships, finances, church, where we live and more. However, some of our decisions turn out to be the absolute worse. If we knew then what we know now, we wouldn't have made them. Instead, we would have trusted God rather than rushing the process and thinking we know everything.

And don't you dare let what people say be the final declaration of who you will be. Your validation and approval doesn't come from them. Your approval comes from God Almighty. Many of the people who criticize you are still trying to figure out their own purpose in life. So don't fret or be disheartened. The One who created you is the only One who can define you.

Your identity and value are found in Christ alone. He calls you His child, friend, and masterpiece. We face so much pressure each day living up to other people's expectations and worrying about what they think about us. Some people in your life know your potential but refuse to let you live it out. And the moment you live beyond their limitations is the very moment they will try to declare you have changed or you have moved before your time.

There will always be competing voices who will try to define how we should live and who we are. We constantly battle with how the world sees us, how we see ourselves, and how God sees us. Therefore, it is significant to know what Christ has already said about you. His thoughts towards you will guard against any false identities and labels thrown on you.

You don't have to perform for your identity. You don't have to compete for your identity. God chose you on purpose and for a purpose. In spite of your imperfections, flaws, and shortcomings, your identity in Christ was fortified on the cross. It was sealed and a done deal.

My question to you is, when are you going to believe in yourself like you believe in others? When are you going to push your business like you push others? When are you going to stop allowing your pain to hinder you?

Your pain can literally launch you into purpose. You keep trying to cover up who you truly are because your journey and story are not what they appear to be. It would shock many if they found out, but it would bless that many more.

Don't shrink and wither in silent due to your own insecurities. That's not what God called you to do. He wants you to blossom! God-given identity is the core of your influence in every sphere you walk into. Your insecurity is not your identity. Your brokenness is not your identity. Your abortion is not your identity, and your divorce is not your identity. Your identity has always been hidden in Christ.

Be who God called you to be and do what you were called to do. No one else has the same anointing, power, drive, and audience as you. You are unique and needed. There are people waiting for you to walk freely into what God called you to do! No barriers. No limitations. No hesitation.

Yes, I know you see what your neighbor and mentor is doing, but if you could see the man or woman God has called you to be, you wouldn't want to be anyone else. Love yourself enough to agree with what God said about you. God had already chosen you before the enemy targeted you.

The real issue with your identity can be settled at the cross and in the Word of God. You are a victor – not a victim. What you went through did not change your value. You are still special and of great worth. Wallowing in regret means you have failed to recognize the true purpose in the process.

I can remember how envious, jealous, and bitter I used to be when I compared my life to others while in college. I couldn't believe God created such a jacked-up individual like me but gave other girls long hair, beautiful voices, and nice bodies. I was flabbergasted that He would do that. How come the girl who attended noonday Bible studies and read His Word every now and then had so many issues? It just was not fair!

I felt like a red-headed stepchild who nobody wanted but tolerated. I felt like a bastard child in the spirit. In fact, I was convinced that God had His favorites, and it surely wasn't me.

My identity had been stolen and as I looked at myself in that dream, I couldn't comprehend what had happened. I knew for a fact that the girl I was watching was not herself. I knew she had picked up another identity along the way and portrayed it as her own. Little did she know that her true self wasn't found in a man or someone else's life. It was built on God Almighty who created her.

No matter how much I tried to club, drink, curse like a sailor, or have a nasty attitude towards everyone, it didn't feel right. I didn't fit in, and I knew it. For years, I had heard that I was different. But I didn't want to be different. Being labeled as different came with loneliness and isolation. Who wanted to be around an oddball or someone a little "uncool"?

I ran away from every prophecy surrounding my future, and I looked to the world for my identity. How naïve I was thinking the world could really define me. It actually reminds me of that one time I tried to take my Toyota Camry to a Wal-Mart technician. No shade towards Wal-Mart, but common sense would tell me that even though the technicians may be well-trained and versatile in many different automotive areas, they don't have all the answers for all car problems.

When I tried to drop my car off at Tire & Lube Express, they politely referred me to the manufacturer, Toyota. It is not that they did not feel equipped to do the job, but they understood their identity. They knew the importance of staying in their lane. Instead of possibly creating further problems, they directed me to the creator of the vehicle.

In life, when you don't know who you are or to whom you belong, it is very likely you will go around mountain after mountain repeatedly asking everyone for assistance and their opinion. Hence, you can't get rid of the never-ending mountain. You keep going to people who didn't create you demanding solutions they can't give.

God never said to reach out to others as the first resort before we turn our focus to Him. The Bible says in Matthew 6:33, "Seek ye first the kingdom of God and His righteousness and all of these things will be added unto you."

Following instructions seems to be harder and harder for us. The Bible is not made up of 66 books just to take up space. Every word written is significant. The predicament many of us face is that we would rather hear words that appease our flesh than those that will save our souls. People tell us what we want to hear, but God speaks with grace and truth.

If I had followed Matthew 6:33 in my self-discovery stage, I would have saved myself a lot of disappointments, heartaches, and misguidance.

> You are a chosen people, a royal priesthood, a holy nation, God's special possession that you may declare the praises of him who called you out of darkness into his wonderful light (1 Peter 2:9).

This verse answers everything you need to know regarding the security of your identity. God Himself has chosen you as a special possession and called you out of darkness into His wonderful light. Hence, you cannot keep looking for validation from the darkness better known as the world.

If we did a survey on Christians desiring the world's validation, I am sure the numbers would be quite shocking. I am confident it would reveal unbelievable figures. We turn to people who are incapable of showing us how to tap into our potential. But also, they can't even pull out the potential and greatness that lies within themselves.

The world's influence creates a false identity and causes you to eventually lose sight of your true worth and identity. Gradually, you will dummy down your true abilities, gifts, and purpose because you let someone put you in a box you were never created to be in.

What you have inside you can free your own family or an entire generation. So there is no time for you to compromise, be comfortable or mediocre. It is quite selfish not to operate in your fullness because each one of us possesses something unique that someone else in the world needs.

The Bible tells us in the Book of Jonah that God instructed Jonah to go to Nineveh and warn them that God could no longer overlook their wickedness. However, Jonah didn't want to go because he knew that the people would repent and that God would show mercy to them and forgive them.

Instead of following the instructions, Jonah decided to run away from God by paying a fare and getting on a ship that was headed in the opposite direction to Tarshish.

This resulted in God sending a violent wind over the sea that was powerful enough to cause damage to the ship. The sailors onboard were afraid and began to cry to their gods and throw their cargo overboard to lighten the ship's load. Eventually, Jonah confessed that he was the cause of the storm and advised them to throw him overboard. Once they threw him overboard, the sea became calm and The Lord sent a big fish to swallow Jonah and he was inside the fish for three days and three nights.

God then spoke to Jonah a second time advising him to journey to Nineveh and deliver the message that he was given. Jonah obeyed God's instructions and warned the people that the city would be overthrown in forty days. The people took heed to the warning, fasted and God showed mercy, compassion and did not destroy the city.

Jonah put innocent people's lives at stake due to his own disobedience. And many of us are rebuking the winds, storms, and wave that are coming in our lives when in reality you don't need to be rebuking, you need to be obeying.

Every storm and attack you are facing is not from the enemy, in fact, many are permitted by God or simply initiated by you. Stop blaming the devil for the consequences of your disobedience.

There will be times in your life when you don't want to do what God has called you to do for many reasons. But whether you agree with it or not, it is non-negotiable. You can't even transfer it to someone who you think is more qualified or equipped. The load and burden of the assignment will lift when you get in position and just obey.

You have to have a "YES" to God that is non-negotiable and unwavering. One that is not tossed to and fro based on circumstances, calamities or emotions. Your prosperity, power, and anointing is connected to your ability to fulfill your God-given assignment.

You may be facing storms in your life because you are running from your calling to use your gifts, preach, prophesy, teach and evangelize all for the glory of God. Whether you know it or not, God will get the glory one way or another and He will cause your life to become uncomfortable until your actions line up with His will and instructions for your life.

This also means that you may have to toss some people off of your ship. It is important that you have people on board that will encourage and push you to be all that God has called you to be. You must have discernment when it comes to allowing people to board your ship even if they have the money to pay the fare. My granddaddy said, "all money ain't good money".

**I Know Who I Am**

When you can positively identify who you are in Christ, there will be no room for who you are to be mistaken. You will no longer have to mimic someone else or dim your lights to make others feel comfortable. You will stand out because you have a sense of peace, joy, and ease that comes with knowing you.

If your identity is not rooted in Christ, conformation to the world becomes inevitable. You will live according to the false expectations and labels others put on you. Your purpose in life should be your number one priority. God doesn't bless copy cats. He only blesses who He originally called and predestined you to be. You can fool people, but you can't fool God. As much as you try to put on and be someone else, people are actually just waiting to love the authentic you.

The day you truly walk in all of who you are, nothing you do will feel as if it has been forced on you. Rather, it will be a joy. You will start tapping into the wisdom, revelation, and power of God that has always been hidden inside of you. The creative juices will flow, you will find yourself thriving in your zone, and others will notice instantly.

Regrettably, we often find ourselves stuck in a place of inadequacy because we focus on every flaw and possible failure that might be on the journey. Many have rejection issues due to Daddy and Mommy wounds. You had to perform for their attention and perfection became your best friend. So now, you believe you have to be perfect for God or perform for His attention.

In the Bible, Moses is the perfect example of someone who battled an identity crisis and nitpicked every flaw. Moses was born in Egypt and during the time of his birth, Pharaoh had ordered that all newborn Hebrew boys be killed. Pharaoh was worried that if the Israelite males kept increasing, they would outnumber him and ally with other Egyptian enemies.

Knowing this, Moses' mother put him in a little handmade boat on the Nile River. Pharaoh's daughter found him and took him in as her own.

I am sure that as Moses became older, he started to

ask questions and noticed that there was a difference between him and the Egyptians with whom he was raised.

In searching out truth and unanswered questions, Moses discovered he was an Israelite and decided to follow God's instructions to bring relief to His people who were Pharaoh's slaves (Hebrews 11:24-25).

While he was minding his own business, God got Moses' attention through a burning bush. He told Moses He saw the distress and suffering the children of Israel were experiencing in Egypt. He wanted to rescue them from the hand of the Egyptians and take them into a land flowing with milk and honey.

I am pretty sure that all of this sounded good to Moses and he was down for it, most likely because He thought God was coming to the rescue. Boy was he wrong. God decided that instead of rescuing the Israelites Himself, He would use Moses, one of their own, to do the honor.

Immediately, Moses came up with all kinds of excuses why he couldn't successfully deliver. First, he basically said, "God do you know who I am? Who am I that I should go down to Pharaoh and bring the Israelites out of Egypt?" (Exodus 3:11).

**Identity Crisis #1** – Moses didn't come into agreement with what God had seen in his life. Anytime God calls us to a thing, it is for a reason. He has equipped you for such a time as this. Your failure to see yourself in all of the greatness God created in you takes nothing away from what God sees in you but keeps you bound to your old identity.

Moses' response meant absolutely nothing to God.
God let him know He would be with him during the entire process. As if that wasn't a good enough answer, Moses then said, "Okay, God! So let's say that I do decide to go through with your plan for my life and head down to rescue the Israelites from Egyptian bondage. If I tell them that the God of your fathers has sent me to you, and they ask me, 'What is his name?' What do I tell them?"

**Identity Crisis #2** – Moses was more concerned about what people had to say than what the Father was saying. This is common in the church because instead of trying to please God, we are more worried about what others will say. Moses showed that he wasn't secure in who his Father was, which demonstrated he wasn't secure in who he was yet.

God continued to be patient with Moses as He is with us. He made sure He answered all of Moses' questions. As you continue to read Exodus Chapters 3 and 4, you can see that Moses' excuses continued.

In Exodus 4:11, he is concerned that the people won't listen to him or believe him. God gives him pointers on how to deal with the people if this happens, but Moses was on to another excuse. Finally, Moses says, "Well, God, I can't speak well. I stutter." Let me remind you that at this point, we are two chapters in and Moses still hasn't found full assurance in God. God then decides to have Moses take Aaron with him to speak on His behalf. He uses the two in a mighty way.

A lot of us identify with Moses because we behave just like him. We never run out of excuses because we refuse to believe God would choose someone like us to be glory carriers on the earth.

**Identity in Christ**

Your identity in Christ has nothing to do with how perfect you are. Ephesians 1:5 gives us hope that "He predestined us for adoption to sonship through Jesus Christ, in accordance with his pleasure and will." It is God's will that we would be His sons and daughters. He has already identified us as His own. Forget what someone said about you. Forget how you or others have labeled you. Even forget circumstances with loved ones that have changed how you see yourself. Your identity doesn't come from people who failed to recognize your value.

Also, do not be identified by the mistakes you made in your past. Rejection and shame, in general, have a way of keeping us in bondage to false identities. Once you become a Christian according to Romans 10:9, you are a new creature in Christ, the old things (identity) have passed away and you can rejoice in the new (2 Corinthians 5:17).

The new includes how God sees you and what He says about you. You are no longer defined by the opinions of others or by your own emotions. Your identity no longer comes from the house you live in, the job you have, the car you drive or your relationship status on social media. Your only concern should be what God says about you.

Knowing and accepting your true identity will change the trajectory of your life. You are the most dangerous to the enemy when you know who you are in Christ.

## **Spiritual Assessment**

Today, make the decision to walk in Holy Ghost boldness and come into agreement with all God has called you to be. You are God's handpicked masterpiece needed in the kingdom. So anytime your thoughts try to convince you that you are anything but what God says you are, cancel those thoughts with the Word of God.

When the enemy tries to discourage you declare the following:

- I am a child of God and a fellow heir with Christ (John 1:12/Romans 8:17)
- I am accepted by Christ (Romans 15:17)
- I am a friend of Jesus (John 15:15)
- I am justified and redeemed (Romans 3:24)
- I am a treasured possession (Deut 7:6)
- I am fearfully and wonderfully made (Psalm 139:14)
- I am the head and not the tail (Deut 28:13)
- I am the apple of His eye (Psalm 17)
- I am the light of the world (Matthew 5:17)

Stop walking around being vulnerable to other people's opinions of you. God created you for a particular purpose. The moment you realize this is the moment you begin changing the world by empowering the people around you.

# Chapter 3
# Internal Examination

Search me, God and know my heart; test me and know my anxious thoughts (Psalm 139:23).

Ever since I was a child, I have loved playing different games such as Sorry, Monopoly, Twister, Connect Four and UNO. It's not only because I enjoy spending time with my family and friends, but I also love challenging myself and adding another win to my column for bragging rights. My competitive spirit, which I am still praying about, is always in full effect. I'm a sports lover with four brothers; what do you expect?

The thought of losing, in any capacity, never sat well with me. If your family is anything like mine, they operate with a spirit of pettiness. That means if you lose, you will never hear the end of it.

As a child, I learned to go into every game with a strategic plan. It was that serious. I put on my game face and hardly talked while playing. Partially because I was already losing badly and had a major attitude or I was simply concentrating on my next move. Concentration is important in any game, especially the board game that demands it by the name of, "Operation."

In the game "Operation," you are a doctor who operates on the patient, Cavity Sam. Cavity Sam lies down on an operation table and his chest is cut open in hopes that someone will successfully remove all of his wacky illnesses with a tweezer. There are 11 ailments inside his chest including a broken heart, headache, frostbite, and a gamer's thumb. The person who successfully removes the most ailments wins. Sounds easy, right? Wrong!

There's always a catch in concentration games like this one. The catch is that you have to be very intentional because the ailments are usually put in odd places. If you touch the sides of an opening, the buzzer will sound off, lighting up Cavity Sam's red nose. When that happens, you lose your turn. However, whether you win or lose, the game is fun overall.

The general concept of "Operation" reminds me of an autopsy in regards to the exposed chest. In an autopsy, once the medical examiners successfully make a positive identification of the deceased, they prepare to perform an internal examination. Before the examination begins, generally, a "body block" is placed under the back of the body. This allows the arms and neck to fall backward so the chest stretches out and pushes upward in an attempt to make it easier to cut open.

Once the body is in the proper position, the chest is exposed with a Y-shaped incision, which starts at the top of each shoulder and runs down to the front of the chest meeting at the lower point of the sternum. This allows the organs to be exposed and removed for further examination. The organs are inspected to see if there is evidence of trauma or other indications that may give the cause of death.

The medical examiners generally use shears or a scalpel when opening the chest to ensure that the heart and lungs are not damaged or disturbed by the cut.

When inspecting the organs, examiners often look at the condition of the heart to ensure there are no adhesions or injuries to the heart. Also, the heart is inspected to determine if any heart diseases could have been the potential cause of death.

## The Condition of the Heart

The condition of the physical heart is important because it pumps blood throughout the body. A person's circulatory system supplies oxygen and nutrients to the tissue in a person's body. It also removes carbon dioxide and carries away waste. Often times, a person's blood and oxygen flow could be blocked resulting in death.

As Christians, it is imperative to conduct heart checks on a regular basis and perform internal examinations. This is essential for daily living in the natural, as well as spiritual. In the natural, when we go to the doctor for a check-up, one of the first things he or she does is test the heart for a normal heartbeat. This is to ensure there is no irregular activity. It is no different from checking our hearts from a spiritual perspective.

The heart is the source of thinking, feeling, will, and emotions. God is concerned about your heart. In our physical bodies, the irregular activity can be tied to multiple ailments and one of them is heart disease. Studies show that heart disease is one of the leading causes of death. Likewise, spiritual heart disease will cause many Christians to suffer from blockages and a poor quality of life. Or in some cases, they will die spiritually.

Maybe you suffered a loss. Perhaps you started hanging around the wrong crowd, experienced failure, disappointment or even heartbreak that damaged your heart. Now, your heart is weak, vulnerable, and you are emotionally unbalanced. You are mentally drained. This causes your emotions, thoughts, and will to be completely altered for the worst.

Think about it. Have you lost your temper with your spouse, parent, coworker, child or a random stranger? Did you recently go to bed angry without trying to reconcile the problem? What about your attitude? Is it nasty and rude, needing improvement after you mistreated someone all in the name of having a bad day?

This is most likely due to your heart issues.

You would think our love for God wouldn't allow us to operate this way. However, often times, we are unable to control our emotions or claim the victory in these situations. This is so because the things we have exposed our hearts to have hindered the flow of the Holy Spirit from entering or going out.

> A good man brings good things out of the good stored up in his heart, and an evil man brings evil things out of the veil stored up in his heart. For the mouth speaks what the heart is full of (Luke 6:45).

When the Holy Spirit is not allowed to freely flow within our hearts and lives, we find ourselves lacking the evidence of the fruit of the Spirit (love, joy, peace, kindness, gentleness, and self-control) in our lives.

Everything we have allowed to enter our hearts outside of God will be revealed through our thoughts, conversations, and actions. Therefore, it is vital to guard our hearts against any thoughts or activities that could block the Holy Spirit from flowing through us. The Bible is full of scriptures concerning the heart that reminds us that everything flows from it. It is literally the core of our very being.

> Above all else, guard your heart, for everything you do flows from it (Proverbs

4:23).

Failure to guard our hearts leaves an open space for the enemy, manipulation, and deception to creep in. Before we know it, backsliding, failure, disappointment, and regret appear all because we neglected to do our due diligence. An unguarded heart is vulnerable to being consumed by unnecessary traffic. Negligence prevents your heart from receiving the proper nutrients needed to fight off the toxins, negativity or lies of the enemy. To be healed and restored, open-heart surgery is required so a spiritual heart transplant can be done.

> I will give you a new heart and put a new spirit in you; I will remove from you your heart of stone and give you a heart of flesh. (Ezekiel 36:26)

If many of us were put on the operating table to undergo a spiritual autopsy or open-heart surgery, the reports would show our hearts have been damaged, infected, and broken. Ultimately, a broken heart is an open and exposed heart. Nevertheless, even when our hearts are shattered into pieces, God draws closer, not leaving us to battle the pain alone or heal in our own strength.

Psalm 51:17 tells us God is close to those who have a broken heart and a contrite spirit. Your weakness allows God to be strong on your behalf. The problem is that instead of letting our hearts be restored and healed, we jump off the operating table too soon. This action exposes the open wounds and possibly makes our hearts, emotions, and thoughts prone to infections. Most won't even allow their bodies to hit the operating table because they have covered up their issues. Their band-aids, which were supposed to start as temporary fixes serve as permanent solutions.

If you know anything about a band-aid, it eventually loses its adhesion and effectiveness after a while. Once the adhesive has become worn, the band-aid will fall off and reveal the bleeding, as well as the scab underneath. You may have thought the cut was healed, but it was merely covered. Sadly, we do this with our lives. We try to cover our hearts' issues and flaws with masks, productivity, and sweeping them under the rug. But at some point, we have to stop trying to hide and learn how to face and endure the process because avoiding it doesn't heal it.

We try so hard to do quick fixes or to alleviate the pain by self-medication with self-pleasure, sex, alcohol, marijuana, material things and so forth. However, these only increase the pain in our hearts and put it out of control.

It is imperative that you allow the surgeon (God) to have access to your heart on the operating table so that He can cut away the excess and stitch you back up. The spiritual cuts and rebukes from our leaders, mentors and the Holy Spirit may not always feel good but it is necessary for our growth. You should never trust a leader who applauds your gifts but neglects your soul. The gift is most effective when the soul is at its healthiest.

Our efforts to heal ourselves or put a halt to the pain may very well be the reason many vices have entered our lives. This leads to anxiety and the acceptance of any and everything including our relationships, careers, money, and material possessions. Nothing is wrong with these things; the problem comes when we idolize and pursue them with wrong motives. Hence, instead of controlling them, they control us.

Many can testify God has been faithful to give them just what they asked for, but for whatever reason, when they got it, they worshipped it instead of worshipping Him. It is as if they see God as a genie in a bottle. Once they received what they wanted, He was no longer needed. Eventually, we are so busy with the distractions, we lose sight of the kingdom and just go through the motions. God doesn't bless you with what you have for you to put Him on the back shelf until you need another emergency.

Many people have made the mistake of becoming bitter because God didn't do what they expected. Bitterness then opens the door for jealousy, unforgiveness, and envy to take residence. The result of that is the creation of an obstruction that prevents God from moving as He needs to in our lives.

When you are committed to something and love it,

you are engaged and dedicated to it. You don't just connect to it on an "as needed" or a "conditional" basis.

In a relationship, two people make the decision to commit in order to learn about each other and grow together. They spend quality time together, discovering each other's likes and dislikes in an effort to make each other happy.

"Janay, I pray that you find someone who loves you as much as your Papaw loves me." Those are the words my grandmother said to me while we were discussing my love life and the lack thereof. They have stuck with me ever since. It is public knowledge that my grandfather loves my grandmother so very much. He is committed and loves her with everything in him. She loves him just as much.

They are my reminder that love is an action word. When you love somebody, you show them how much you appreciate them by words of affirmation and your presence. Love is not selfish because it comes from a pure place.

Love is a beautiful thing when both individuals are on the same page. Unfortunately, sometimes in a relationship or friendship, one person is more committed than the other. Often times, it is because we place high expectations and demands on people without communicating them. On the other hand, I have witnessed people who verbally commit, but their actions show otherwise.

These examples remind me of Christians who claim they love God, but their hearts are far from Him. Instead of reading the Word, obeying His commandments and loving others as He has commanded, they do the very opposite.

We have created a cultural mindset that is always looking for a hand out from God. However, we are usually unwilling to even raise our hands in worship to Him. We have created a culture where people are very concerned about what God can do for them, but there is generally no thought about how they can make it a joint effort.

It's as if we want the full-time benefits of being a Christian, but only want to put in part-time hours. Nobody wants to do the work. We want the rewards without the responsibility and the promises without the process. There is no commitment.

Yes, you may post all of this religious and deep stuff on Facebook, but truth be told, you haven't read one scripture all month, which is a tell-tale sign that you haven't committed.

A real sincere encounter with God will motivate you to seek His face and want more of Him. There should be a heart transformation that takes place in His presence – a heart transplant if you will.

> As water reflects the face, so one's life reflects the heart (Proverbs 27:19).

## Internal Examination

If you say you have been in the face of God but there has been no outward change from your inner transformation, something is wrong. Some would say you are making false claims because what you have done in private will eventually come out in public.

Sad to say, so many people's hearts are turned very far from God and the further they move away from Him, the more they backslide. The more they find themselves outside of the will of God, the more their attitudes stink. The heart transformation is not a once a year process; it has to be a consistent renewing.

I learned from personal experience that spending time with God early in the morning made my day much smoother and less stressful. I had the morning scripture hidden in my heart. That way if my coworkers got on my nerves or something didn't go my way, I was still in a good place. I would shift to the positive so my day would not take a turn for the worst.

But the opposite is also true. It's like taking a bath. If you don't take a bath daily, you will begin to stink. You can try to put deodorant on top of the old deodorant to cover up the funk, but you will still stink. And the worst thing a person can do is try to spray cologne or perfume on top of a disgusting smell. Eww! Have you ever smelled that? It still stinks, but it's worse.

Can you imagine that smell? It's exactly what happens to your life when you don't take a spiritual bath or allow the Holy Spirit to move freely within you to create a clean heart daily.

When you don't shower in the Word or use the scriptures as soap, it will show. You will start to stink in the nostrils of God. Your attitude will stink. Your patience will run very thin, and you will walk around like a ticking time bomb just waiting to explode. You wake up saying, "Today isn't the day" or "I wish somebody would." (You may laugh while reading this because you can testify that was or is you.)

You walk around waiting for somebody to do one thing wrong to you and then BAM! The spirit of offense manifests, and you go off on everybody. And you think because you are offended, that you are right. Not necessarily. In reality, what you are doing is forcing everyone else to pay for your lack of obedience and commitment to God. And God forbid your poor actions come into contact with a non- believer who is looking for you to be an example.

**A Heart Check**

When you find yourself wavering from God, you need to be honest and ask yourself, "Why is my heart so far from God?" The answer to this question can change the entire trajectory of your walk.

What stopped you from being surrendered to God and prevents you from enjoying the things of God? Be honest with yourself. Don't think that just because you attend church every time the doors are open, you don't need a heart check. I know plenty of Christians who attend church as much as humanly possible but raise more hell than anybody else because their hearts are filthy and turned away from God. You can backslide right there in the pews.

> These people come near to me with their mouth and honor me with their lips, but their hearts are far from me. Their worship of me is based on merely human rules they have been taught. (Isaiah 29:13)

These Christians go to church Sunday after Sunday, serve on every committee, and probably sing on the praise team. I applaud servitude, but we can't get so caught up in what we do for the church that we fail to be the church. Jesus could care less about how much you are at church if your heart doesn't bear the fruits of a Christian. There is nothing wrong with being a faithful church member, but what are the motives behind it and more importantly, what does your heart resemble?

**EXAMPLE A:** Mike attends church regularly but does not display love and is nasty to everyone.

**EXAMPLE B:** Betty works every other Sunday so she is only able to attend two services a month. But while working as a nurse, she displays the fruit of the Spirit, allowing the Holy Spirit to lead and guide her actions and thoughts on the job.

After the examination, which heart resembles one

of a Christian and which one appears to need open heart surgery?

In Matthew 23, Jesus read the Pharisees their entire receipts when they continuously tried to openly rebuke Him for the miracles and acts He performed on the earth. He called them hypocrites in verse 27 because He said they looked, acted, and even talked saved, but they were not saved. They had religion but no relationship. They just knew how to play the part. Sounds familiar?

Jesus said they were like "whitewashed tombs – beautiful on the outside but filled on the inside with dead people's bones and all sorts of impurity." In verse 28, He goes on to say that while outwardly they look like righteous people, inwardly, their hearts were filled with hypocrisy and lawlessness.

At this point, I am sure Jesus had just about enough with people playing a part they didn't even audition for. He wanted to make it clear that He wasn't concerned about how much people looked saved if their hearts didn't match it. Sure you have a faithful Sunday school record, but you have a filthy life. Where are your fruits?

Galatians 5:22-23 identifies nine attributes that show visible "fruit of the Spirit." We have to let our spiritual hearts line up with what God originally intended for us, His children.

> But be doers of the word and not hearers only, deceiving yourself. (James 1:22)

We can become so religious by getting caught up in the traditions of serving and attending church that we lose sight of the truth that God is concerned about our hearts and relationships with Him.

We serve so much thinking it will get us a first-class ticket into heaven, but we refuse to pause and get a word from our pastor that will transform our lives. Then we have the audacity to say God isn't speaking to us. How can we expect Him to speak if we never slow down enough to hear what He is trying to say to us?

In Luke 10:38-42, we see that Martha has a servant's heart and she enjoys serving Jesus. She ministers to Jesus' physical needs. I have been in church for a while, and I always hear Martha catching slack when it comes to service because people compare her to her sister Mary who always finds herself at the feet of Jesus.

I am not against Martha serving completely because serving is an important principle of a Christian, which gives us another opportunity to be like Jesus. However, what we have to understand is that there is a time to serve and a time to sit. While somebody is receiving from Jesus, somebody has to be anointed enough to serve.

Serving is necessary because the more God pours out to us while we are sitting at His feet, the more we will be able to pour out to others.

The important thing that many miss is there is a balance that comes with serving and sitting. You have to know your season to sit and your season to serve. Martha became so busy she wasn't getting spiritually fed. This is what happens to many of us and why we are in the spiritual shape we are in.

After you do your part in leading prayer, worship or playing the instrument, you tap out and plug into social media or even exit the building until it is your time to be used again. These types of actions are selfish, not only to others but also to God. When we do this, we are really saying there is no room for growth or we are just not interested.

God never promised to save us by our works or our volunteer hours at church.

> For it is by grace you have been saved, through faith---- and this is not from yourselves, it is the gift of God—not by works, so that no one can boast (Ephesians 2:8-9).

You are not called or chosen because of your works. There is not enough that you can do to gain more of God's attention. You already have it. He is just looking for your willingness to serve with a pure and clean heart. He is looking for people who are willing to walk in the love and ways of God.

In 1 Samuel 16, God sent the prophet Samuel on a mission to Jesse's house to anoint one of his sons as the king to replace Saul. He tried to pick one of the seven sons that Jesse introduced based on their appearance.

## Internal Examination

God quickly let Samuel know that when trying to choose a king, he shouldn't be so concerned about what the person looked like or how tall he was because God Himself rejected potential kings because of this.

God advised Samuel that although man looks at the outward appearance when determining their next king, He observes the inward part of a man. He is impressed by the heart when picking a king.

The Bible shows us that all of Jesse's boys were rejected as king except for David. Interestingly, David was not initially mentioned by Jesse because to him, David was more of a servant than a son. But God saw David as a king because His heart spoke volumes.

What does your heart look like? What does it say about you? It doesn't matter what people know you as or how many titles you have. God could care less about what platforms you stand on Sunday after Sunday if you have no power or anointing.

One of the worst things a ministry leader can do is have an unchecked heart because it will show outwardly. You can be an usher at the front door with a disgusting attitude and run every visitor away from the church. Now, you have messed up their perspective of the church and possibly God before they even entered the sanctuary. At this point, the worship team and pastor have no way to gain this person's heart, attention or soul because of unchecked holes and problems in your heart.

You can be a pastor or preacher who is mad because the offering wasn't what you wanted it to be, so you preach from an angry heart on the pulpit. God is not pleased and neither should we be. It is time that we turn our hearts back to God.

He doesn't care if you make six figures a year or if you are one of the church's largest tithers if you aren't giving with pure motives and a grateful heart. God wants a sacrificial and generous heart. What we give and how we give it are mere reflections of our hearts.

**The Root of the Heart Blockage**

If the things that have affected us are not correctly identified and dealt with, they can lead to other problems in the body. What is preventing the Holy Spirit from freely-flowing in your life? Is it fear, shame, hate, envy, bitterness or unforgiveness? All of these characteristics have an effect on how much access God has to our hearts. They influence us to turn from God and choose our own way. Many Christians have major problems when it comes to forgiving those who betrayed their trust in some form or fashion. Unforgiveness builds in the heart. I get it! Trust me, I do, but unforgiveness is one of the worst things you can carry around in your heart because it puts a barrier between you, God, and those around you. A life marked with bitterness and unforgiveness not only develops trust issues, but it also blocks you from being heard and forgiven by God.

## Internal Examination

> For if you forgive other people when they sin against you, your heavenly Father will also forgive you. But if you do not forgive others their sins, your Father will not forgive your sins. (Matthew 6:14-15)

The acts of forgiving and being forgiven are inseparable. Unforgiveness hinders you from receiving forgiveness from God until you complete the instructions given in Matthew 6:14-15 about forgiving others. It doesn't mean the offense, hurt, pain or betrayal didn't happen and that it should be ignored. Rather, it is saying you should trust God to be God enough to handle it.

The inability to forgive is more dangerous than many would like to admit. It has the power to make you physically sick and throw your focus off. You stay up all night upset about the offense, checking the offender's Facebook and Instagram pages, while the offender has gone on living his or her best life, just like you should be doing.

Some people have held grudges for years. The reality is many don't even know why they were mad in the first place. If this unforgiveness is not dealt with head-on and you fail to press beyond it, you will forfeit your God-given blessings and inheritance.

Forgiving someone doesn't mean you are weak or you are letting the person off the hook. Forgiveness impacts you more than them. If you continue to focus on what they did to you, you will miss what God is trying to do for you. Just like Jesus provided grace and mercy to us, we too must extend the same mercy to others.

God is not like man. His love for us is unconditional. He wants us to experience and demonstrate that same love on earth, but we can't if we continue to harbor resentment in our hearts.

> Get rid of all bitterness, rage, and anger, brawling and slander, along with every form of malice. Be kind and compassionate to one another, forgiving each other, just as in Christ God forgave you (Ephesians 4:31- 32).

You will find once you release the bitterness, your heart will not only be made right, but it will be lighter as well. No longer will you carry around the weight, baggage or toxins that were once there. And the harsh reality is that a lot of people need to put their pride to the side and provide a much-needed apology. Ego partnered with pride has kept many from divine and meaningful connections due to the inability to be the bigger person and say that they got it wrong. It may not automatically result in reconciliation, but at least the opportunity for forgiveness will be presented.

Some people may never accept the apology and then there are those who will never give an apology.

However, you have to learn the importance of forgiving others even when they aren't sorry for what they did.

Forgiveness is the key that will unlock the door to abundant life if you learn to do it quickly. The key will unbolt the handcuffs of resentment and open the door for the newness of God to enter.

As much as we think we know better, it is only God who can heal the recesses of our souls. He is the Great Physician with the cure you have been looking for. It will complete your healing and recovery. You don't have to walk around with an unchecked heart full of bitterness, resentment, hatred, and anger. You don't have to let a hardened heart erect a barrier between you and your heavenly Father.

Once you hand over your heart to Him, He can transform it to look like His. That will allow Him to trust you with specific blessings in the spiritual realm that a fragile heart can't handle properly. Your inward change will then begin to resonate outwardly.

## **Spiritual Assessment**

It is crucial that you do a heart check on a daily basis. Ask God to search your heart and reveal the things that taint it so they can be removed.

What in your heart has caused you to be far from God? What in your life can be a hindrance in the future if not dealt with?

1. Issues with your parents

2. Failure in relationships, friendships or marriage

3. Feeling like God let you down

4. Abandonment

5. Rejection

Whatever it is, be honest and open. Write down the issues. Journal them.

This will be the start of an exchange from your heart that will allow God to apply the scalpel and create a new heart in you.

# Chapter 4
# Mind Control

> For as he thinks in his heart, so is he. "Eat and drink!" he says to you, But his heart is not with you." (Proverbs 23:7 NKJV).

I remember being baptized when I was younger. Probably in elementary or middle school. The amazing thing is that my grandfather, who was my pastor at the time, baptized me and my cousins together. It was a great experience. We had a firm foundation, and we were talked to about what baptism meant before we were baptized. But sure enough, I still came out of the water a smart-mouthed little girl with the sassiest attitude.

After I got older, I began to develop an intimate relationship with God. I made the decision to rededicate my life to Christ and get baptized again. Not because it was required but because it was more symbolic to me.

I remember calling my Papaw before I came home for the Christmas break, and I explained my decision to him. He was excited! We scheduled the baptism for January 6, 2008.

I recall like yesterday how excited I was. It was as if I was turning over a new leaf and becoming a completely new young lady. Everyone was very supportive, but only a few were honest about what I was getting into.

I knew I was going to be held to a higher standard. One of my mentors was honest with me letting me know it was one of the best steps I could ever make in life, but it would not come without a cost. She explained to me that my commitment to God would make the enemy come after me even harder. He would do so because my testimony and the anointing that rested on my life would annihilate the plans of hell. She said God was going to empower me to help others find freedom. Thus, the enemy would be angry because of it. She was 100% correct!

The enemy started to attack everything around me once I made the decision to surrender to God, as well as the plans and purposes He had for my life. It was a constant battle in my relationships, money, and spiritual journey. Throughout his onslaughts, the fiercest attacks were on my mind.

In the midst of my decision making on a bad day, Satan would try to plant thoughts of negativity and defeat. He would say things like, "You were better off in the world" or "If God loved you like He says He does, why does He let you suffer?" Although these lies tried to penetrate, I committed to the process. I continued to speak the Word of God and applied it to my life.

It is very important when making your commitment to living for God that you start with your mind. Romans 12:2 instructs us not to conform to the pattern of the world but be transformed by the renewing of our minds. Then we will be able to test and approve what God's will is – His good, pleasing, and perfect will.

When we maintain our old way of thinking, refuse to bask in God's presence and meditate on His words to renew our minds daily, we are subject to think and act as the world does. This is why many people have found themselves in backslidden states. They do not go through the process of mind renewal. They allow their minds to constantly replay past failures and defeats. Before they know it, they have thought themselves into feeling they deserve the predicament or trials they are in.

In the book of Genesis, the Bible tells us that Adam and Eve were deceived when the enemy came to Eve in the form of a serpent. He convinced her that if she ate from the tree of knowledge, she would gain great insight into what God was trying to keep from her. She fell for it. She was deceived and so was Adam. The enemy knew she wasn't strong enough to outwit what he was trying to accomplish, which eventually led to the fall of man.

Paul talked about this in 2 Corinthians 11:3 saying, "But I am afraid that just as Eve was deceived by the serpent's cunning, your minds may somehow be led astray from your sincere and pure devotion to Christ."

What is leading your mind astray from sincere and pure devotion to God? Is it lack of finances? Your waiting that seems in vain? Your mistakes and failures? Your sin you have so easily committed? We have to be able to identify what is keeping our minds so lost in the sauce we can't even focus on the things of God.

Christ gives us fair warning throughout the Bible concerning the enemies' tactics and his schemes. Unfortunately, we slack up and think that a thought is just a thought. We don't realize that one thought can send us right into a depression.

See, when the enemy gets a hold of your mind, he will start making you think everyone is against you; you will never be anything good; you will always be broke, and you will never amount to anything. He will attack your mind relentlessly until you become mentally bound.

When some people think of a prison, their first image is a huge, enclosed facility with jail cells and security bars. They view it as a place full of criminals, but I would suggest otherwise. Franklin D. Roosevelt once said, "Men are not prisoners of fate, but only prisoners of their own minds." Too many of us have allowed our thoughts to hold us hostage.

What you think will eventually become your reality. If you look at your situation and say you will always be broke, then that is what you will be. If you feel God is taking too long to get you a mate and you speak that, you will always be single. You will self-sabotage any blessing that tries to come into your life.

But the very opposite is also true. Sometimes you have to speak a thing until you see a thing. You have to train your mind to think on things that are pure, true, and admirable. Even when you see a doctor's report that is bad, you have to train your mind to think you are healed. When you need to start your business, but you have no money, you have to believe God will supply all your needs.

Your words are powerful. That's why the Bible tells us, "Death and life are in the power of our tongues." Your words and thoughts will either keep you stuck or force you to come out of a dead place. God didn't create us to have stinking thinking even when our situations don't look favorable. You must have enough strength not to let your situation corrupt your thinking. Corrupt thinking clouds your vision, which reflects on your focus that is crucial to your future.

I learned very quickly that the enemy is very cunning and deceitful in his actions. He knows that if he can get into your mind, he can eventually assist you in being the detriment of your future. He plants seeds that will produce weeds of lies instead of flowers of truth if you allow it.

> For though we walk in the flesh, we do not war after the flesh; For the weapons of our warfare

are not carnal, but mighty through God to the pulling down of strong holds; Casting down imaginations, and every high thing that exalts itself against the knowledge of God, and bringing into captivity every thought to the obedience of Christ (2 Corinthians 10:3-5 KJV).

You have to pull down the strongholds the strongman has planted in your mind. Every thought that is not of God has to be cast down.

> Let this mind be in you, which was also in Christ Jesus (Philippians 2:5).

Nothing we are experiencing is worse than anything Jesus experienced. However, His mindset throughout every encounter produced a favorable outcome. The enemy feeds on victim mentalities.

If you think you can't, then you won't. If you think you can, then you will. It's a simple concept of the power of mindset and perspective. And if you change your perspective, it will change your life. Your mind is a powerful battlefield and in it lies your thoughts. Inevitably, your mind will be attacked from the moment you wake up in the morning.

When I was a child, I was expected to make up my bed before doing anything else. That is exactly how we should be concerning our minds. We must make it a priority to control our minds and thoughts from the get-go every morning.

It would be a shame if we let the enemy creep into

our thoughts because we are careless enough to leave them unguarded. The mind is a war ground, and the enemy is suited and ready to go to war against the things of God concerning you.

I wish my testimony was that the enemy never gained access to my mind, but that isn't my story.

The first time he launched an attack was during my freshman semester in college. At this particular time, mental health wasn't talked about openly. It was still a very private and embarrassing thing to have mental challenges. I began taking anti-depressant medication after seeing a psychiatrist. However, because I have a praying family who believes the name of Jesus cures everything down to my mental state, I was off those medications immediately.

For almost eight years, I lived a life full of faith, hope, and freedom in my mind and every area of my life. And then a storm came. Its winds and waves battered my life; the impact was harsh and hard.

After being content with my eight years of singleness, God offered me the opportunity to begin dating again. This led to a relationship, an engagement, and I just knew I had finally met the one. It started as a breath of fresh air accompanied by butterflies and big smiles at the top of the relationship. Of course, no relationship is perfect, but even in the rough moments, God really showed me His love and concern for me throughout. Unfortunately, the butterflies and big smiles eventually turned into red flags, non-stop tears, heartbreak, and betrayal.

It was a fairytale that turned into a nightmare. So much so the conversations and inquiries about our wedding plans and save the date invitations made me cringe. I knew the truth that no one else could see. Beneath my mask and Facebook posts was despair. I had to face the reality that what I thought I wanted wasn't necessarily what I needed. Most of all, I knew I had to make a decision that would shock many.

See, I have always been the strong one in many of my circles and my family. But this time, I was weak. Yet, I had to put up a front and pretend I was strong to provide hope to others while covering my man publicly but suffering privately. The more I suffered in silence, the more the enemy started to build strongholds in my mind.

Of course, I was expected to stay in the relationship and make it work. That's what society taught us. As women, we are supposed to go through the worse with a man in order to experience the best. We are supposed to endure the suffering first in order to experience the glory later. But I also knew that some habits and cycles, if not dealt with before marriage, would spring up and create much chaos and death in the relationship resulting in divorce.

I had so many mixed emotions and much pressure on my shoulders. My mind was bogged down with two options: do I stay and just deal with it for the sake of not letting people down? Or do I walk away knowing my value and sticking to my assignment to break the generational curse of infidelity and divorce that has plagued my bloodline?

After much prayer, fasting and personal, as well as pre-marital counseling, I was led by God to call off the engagement and break off the relationship immediately. The wedding was just six months down the road.

Not only was I instructed by God to end it, but I was to make a public announcement via social media that the engagement was off.

Let's just pause here for a moment of silence to my heart that took a 600-feet drop after these instructions and my jaw drop that followed right behind. Like "ummm" come again, God? Can you repeat that because I need to make sure that I heard you right? You want me to do what? And then tell who?"

Privately ending the relationship and calling off the engagement wasn't so bad because I had peace about the decision, and I knew I was in God's will. But I couldn't fathom telling my list of 5,000 Facebook friends and 600 followers that the public relationship they had admired and the wedding they were counting down was no longer happening.

I felt like a complete failure. I felt I had not only failed myself but my family, friends, and those who had hope in a godly relationship through the lenses of our courtship. I was devastated, but I pressed on with the little faith and strength I had as a woman of God knowing that I was in His will. I refused to allow my loyalty to people make me disloyal to God.

In the process of healing, more truths were revealed that solidified I had made the right decision. But questions didn't produce answers fast enough for me and before I knew it, I was met face-to-face with a long lost enemy – depression.

Rumors and lies started to surface, but God wouldn't allow me to open my mouth. I got real raw and vulnerable with God and started to ask questions. "God, why did you allow me to go through this?" "What did I do so bad to deserve this?" "Am I not good enough to be one man's wife?" "Why can't I defend myself?"

I was angry at God because, at that moment, I felt as if He had failed me. I had allowed the enemy to pitch his tent in my mind and made him feel right at home. I allowed every negative thought that appeared in my mind to manifest into my speech and eventually, it consumed me.

I tried to make sense of it, but 1+1 wasn't adding up to 2. In almost no time, I blamed myself for everything and started speaking what I was feeling. My focus was blurred and headspace was congested. At one point, I started to think the pain, shame, and embarrassment were too much to bear. For a moment or two, I thought about ending it all. And like many people who want to end it all, it's not that I really wanted to leave this earth. I just wanted the pain to end and at that moment, I saw no way out. I kept beating myself up and condemnation was the loudest thing in my ear. I needed an escape.

It reminded me of Elijah in 1 Kings Chapter 19. He had killed Jezebel's prophets and right after, she sent for him to be killed. Elijah literally knew he was about to engage in a fight for his life, and he decided to run away. God found him under a juniper tree asking Him to take his life. He said, "I have had enough." After his confession to God, He fell asleep. Here was a man who was just in the limelight of success. Now, he was in a depression and the thought of suicide plagued his mind. God neither granted his request nor condemned him for his honesty. He dealt with his humanity beyond the anointing and assignment.

God sent angels to minister to Elijah. The angels said, "Get up and eat." He ate the bread the angels brought and drank the water before going back to sleep. The angels came back again with the same commandment. However, this time, they told him to get up because the journey was too much for him. Elijah arose again to eat and then journeyed. The Bible said that he was strengthened so that he journeyed for 40 days and 40 nights. He tried to isolate himself in a cave before God called him out, but eventually, he changed his posture and returned to the presence of God.

This goes to show that a little nap and some food can go a long way. When was the last time you rested? When was the last time you had a good meal physically and spiritually? A lack of rest can be detrimental to the mind and journey. If you don't properly assess the fatigue, weariness, and hunger that life brings, you will easily forfeit the assignment on your life prematurely.

The words from Jezebel will linger in your mind to intimidate you. You will doubt your ability, anointing, and calling. You will believe the lies and become one with them. The enemy knows the weaknesses that will make you retreat.

Elijah found himself in a cave due to depression. It wasn't that God had left Him. He decided to leave God and the world by isolating himself. And just like Elijah, it's time for you to come out of hiding and seclusion.

You may be in a season of fear, doubt, regret, and darkness, but you have the power and dominion over your emotions. And once you learn this, you will learn that your feelings are not always the facts. It is important that you learn how to discipline and manage your emotions. Decide to change your garments and dress in the garment of praise for the spirit of heaviness. Your darkness is not beyond God's power to heal and restore you. God sent me help just like He sent Elijah. Likewise, He will send you help to get out of that state.

To recover, you will also need people on your team who refuse to attend your pity party and won't let you give up. You must surround yourself with people who see your potential, purpose, and future beyond your present circumstances.

There was a point that depression chose me but then I chose depression. I got complacent and lost all sense of expectation regarding life. Until one day, I decided I wasn't going to die like this. Like Elijah, I got rest, fed my soul with spiritual food, and I demanded my emotions come under subjection to the living God. I started to walk in victory over depression. I got my strength, fight, and mind back. I dug myself out of depression. I pushed that dirt of failure, heartbreak, disappointment, and shame to the side. It tried to bury me alive, but I stood strong in the strength of God and declared I shall live and not die. I tended to my own emotions, happiness, and peace. My mental health and healing became far more valuable to me than anything else.

I admitted I wasn't strong enough, and I didn't have to be. God's strength allowed me to be weak. I no longer wanted to wear my cape or be involved in the Black Superwoman Syndrome. As black women, we are expected to manifest strength, succeed and make it happen by any means necessary.

We become scared of the consequences of admitting that we are hurting and struggling. Scared that we will be looked at as weak because we need help taking care of the kids, cleaning up the house, running the businesses, budgeting the money, paying the bills, and following our dreams. We witnessed our mothers and grandmothers make it happen, so we are expected to do the same. Once I realized I didn't want to carry that weight, I got out of bed daily and made my way to my therapist's couch. I fought against the stereotypes of a black Christian woman, and I gave myself permission to heal.

I was OK coming to grips with the fact that I made bad decisions, didn't have all the answers, didn't have it all together and that I needed help. I stopped suppressing my emotions, and let myself be very vulnerable.

For the first time in years, I put myself first. Sheesh! That was the hardest thing to do. While people were telling me that social media needed me and my encouraging words, I knew I needed me more. I had to do what was necessary to get my life back. I left my stressful and busy career in college athletics and moved to another state. I switched my career to one that was stress-free for the sake of my peace and journey to healing.

I went back to therapy, took a five-month social media hiatus, stopped accepting ministry engagements, balanced out my circle, closed my ear gates and eye gates to things that no longer served my mental health purpose, and I began to thrive where I once survived.

I embraced the season of isolation and alone time with God and started to evolve into who God created me to be. Life wasn't about the title of preacher, prophet or intercessor. None of that meant more than reacquainting myself with the daughter of the King that I was and embracing Him as my Father. I restarted date nights with God at my coffee shop and even dated myself again. The reality is I had lost myself in the process of trying to please others. However, the peace of God that surpasses all understanding returned, and it consumed my mind and heart. I decided to trust God even when I didn't understand Him. I was convinced it would all make sense after a while. And it did.

I allowed myself to grieve. This was life-changing for me because I had heard about grief as it relates to physical death, but nobody taught me how to process grief from major disappointment. One important lesson I learned while grieving is that those who were there with you in your glory won't necessarily be there for you during your grief.

I lost a lot of friends and associates, but I didn't take it personally. I learned that most of them didn't know (lacked knowledge) how to deal with my grief. Then many just weren't my people to begin with. They were just there for the moment.

In the midst of my journey, I had some good days and then I had some extremely rough days. It was as if I was starting from scratch, but I committed to my process. And I quickly learned to celebrate that process and the fact I had made progress. I was reminded that just because you have a few rough days in your season doesn't mean it isn't still a good season.

Things were gradually beginning to look up, and I was slowly getting my strength and joy back. I still didn't have all of the answers, but I didn't wait until everything fell into place to receive the peace that it would all make sense after a while. Once I accepted the peace of God, life started to line up. I knew if I changed my mind, I would change my life.

You may not know how everything is going to pan out as it is related to your process. Nevertheless, obey and trust God enough that He will not lead you astray. Abraham left his family not knowing where he was going. Sometimes God gives you instructions without every detail, but you must still trust Him, the God of your salvation. And do not expect others to understand.

> By faith Abraham, when called to go to a place he would later receive as his inheritance, obeyed and went, even though he did not know where he was going (Hebrews 11:8).

In my process to healing, God spoke these words in my ear, "My daughter, I am proud of you! You have endured tough times and handled them very well. Surrounded by the darkness, you still found the light and ran to it (Me). What's remarkable is that through it all, you continued to be the light. I am pleased with you."

The tears that rolled down my face were signs of

great relief and victory because no matter how much advice people gave me, their experiences were not mine. I was simply praying that I was doing the right thing, the right way. I despised what was now a part of my story and testimony. The testimony that what was once a beautiful success was now a public failure. The testimony that I almost allowed one man's inability to appreciate, love, and be faithful to me make me doubt any confidence, self-worth, and value I once had. The testimony that I almost came into agreement with the lies of the enemy and whispers of others concerning my present and future. But I saw the light.

Though depression, guilt, regret, and failure overtook me, I somehow managed to focus on the light. I found the strength to never lose my grip on God's promises for me, the words that He had already spoken over me or the ability to hear His voice. Most of all, I never lost sight of God's grace and mercy, which allowed me to forgive others and myself. Freedom and healing immediately became my portion.

Every day, I spoke words of affirmation that I was more than enough. I was beautiful. I was loved. I was capable. I was needed. I was appreciated. I would be the wife of one husband, helpmeet, and biggest supporter. I decided to clap and celebrate my strength, courage, endurance, healing, fight freedom, and "dopeness." Most of all, I patted myself on the back for making a decision that thousands would never have had the guts to make. I literally broke a generational curse. Many of you will break them as well.

The enemy will try his best to bombard your mind and enter through whatever open door, gap or crack he can. He will make every effort to plant seeds of fear, doubt, and your greatest insecurities into your life. However, you have to take control of those thoughts and stop them at the door. The attack will come and the impact may be great, but it won't be able to penetrate the blood of Jesus that protects it.

You may have to change your environment, circles, and speech because it is hard to heal in the place you were hurt in. Trust me, if the enemy is unsuccessful in getting your joy, he will attack you in your environment.

You have to make your environment conducive to your growth and healing. Praise and Worship is one of the keys that makes that possible. Even when your circumstances or journey doesn't appear favorable, your worship, in the midst of it, has the power to cause a shift in the environment and in your healing.

What you are dealing with may not necessarily have been your fault, but the responsibility to heal is yours. Healing is a process, not only for you but for generations after you. You may not know it but people are looking at you as an example of how to heal properly.

One thing I noticed quickly is that I didn't have any boundaries or any self-care tactics in place. I was so used to putting others before me and investing in them that I failed to invest in myself. Self-care is important during the healing process. Having to focus on yourself forces you to put others to the side and pay attention to your needs. You have to examine your mental state all the way down to your physical state. Setting boundaries is a must. Here are a few things that you can do as it relates to self-care:

1. Forgive yourself and be kind to you. Give yourself permission to be happy and show compassion to yourself.

2. Allow others to love you. This is just as important as you loving yourself. Come out of hiding.

3. Schedule certain must-do activities on your calendar monthly such as a movie night, a day to serve others, a day to serve yourself, a date night (even if it's by yourself), a day outside, a day off social media, a lunch date with friends, and exercise

4. Release any memories that will make you relapse into a dark place. This includes pictures, videos, certain music, movies or circles that remind you of the source of your trauma.

5. Accountability is a must. When you are struggling, having a bad thought or at your breaking point, surround yourself with a set of people you can be honest with about your

mental state. People who can be trusted to cover you and pray you through it until you come out of it.

6. Ask for help. Stop being so prideful that you struggle when you don't have to. If you need help with the kids, business efforts, house duties, etc. ask someone for help. You can't carry the load on your own. You were not designed to do so.

Along with the aforementioned, there are other actions you can take to ensure you have a healthy balanced life. Your wholeness will change the course of your life. We can't be good workers, servants, daughters, sons, friends, mothers or fathers to anyone until we are first good to ourselves.

The process may be long but don't rush it before the right time. Make sure that while you are committed, you stop and celebrate your victory, strength, and survival. Don't discount or downplay how much you have actually overcome and grown.

The days you held yourself together and didn't have a breakdown, applaud yourself. Constantly remind yourself of how proud you are about your achievements each step of the way. Don't wait on others to praise you.

Declare you are victorious and more than an overcomer through Jesus Christ. Speak from a heavenly perspective and demand your emotions to submit to the name of Jesus. Declare God is the Lord over your mind, will, and emotions. And declare that you will defeat everything the enemy tries to throw at you and be greater than any obstacle, trauma or mountain that is before you.

## **Spiritual Assessment**

It is time you take control of your mind and stop falling victim to the traps of the enemy. Think about your mind. If the thought doesn't line up with the Word or will of God, it is time to change that and take control. Think about every situation or thought that may influence you to backslide and terminate your commitment to God. Renounce those thoughts and be intentional about renewing, retraining, and guarding your mind every day.

1. **Renew your mind -** We must fill our minds with the Word of God to drown out any negativity, doubt, worry or insecurity. It is an ongoing and daily process that you must be intentional about. You must meditate on the Word day and night. If you practice reading and meditating on the Word, it will saturate your mind. Make sure you read, study, and meditate on the Word of God on your own. Equally important, is receiving sound teaching as well (Psalm 119:15)

2. **Retrain your mind -** When you haven't exercised in a while or used a skill for quite some time, it may take some retraining. It is the same thing with our minds. We must train our minds to the things of God. Once we do this, our perspectives will be shaped by the Word of God, not on the world's view.

    Ensure every thought that comes into your mind is lined up with the Word of God. David said in Psalm 139:23, "Search me, God, and know my heart; test me and know my anxious thoughts." He knew there was a possibility his thoughts were displeasing to God, but he gave God permission to deal with them as He pleased.

3. **Guard your mind -** It is important that after you have renewed and retrained your mind that you are also intentional about guarding what you allow to enter it. Ephesians 6:17 reminds us to put on the helmet of salvation. You have to guard and protect your mind against the thoughts and ideas you entertain. You are not only responsible for what you allow to come in, but it is also your duty to dismiss anything negative that comes to your thoughts. Don't let them settle in. (Philippians 4:8). Evaluate your habits. What do you listen to? What are you watching on a daily basis? What are your thoughts about? How do you start your day off?

4. **Seek Counsel -** I am an advocate for therapy. I think you can love Jesus and still see a therapist. Jesus saved me and therapy played a part in renewing my mind.

Will it be easy? No. But I can promise you that if you can change your thinking, it will indeed change your life. Break out of that prison mentality today by getting rid of that "stinking thinking."

## Chapter 5
## The Struggle Is Real

> I have discovered this principle of life — that when I want to do what is right, I inevitably do what is wrong. I love God's law with my heart. But there is another power within me that is at war with my mind. This power makes me a slave to the sin that is still within me. Who will free me from this life that is dominated by sin and death? (Romans 7: 21-24)

Have you ever had good intentions to do the right thing, but in the end, you did the very opposite?

For instance, you went to bed with your mind set on being on time for work or school, but when that alarm went off, you decided you could use an extra five minutes of sleep. So you hit the snooze button and before you knew it, you had slept an extra 30 minutes. Or maybe you were set on fasting between 6 a.m. and 6 p.m. with your church. You had your mind in the right place but all of sudden, your boss decided he wanted to treat everyone to lunch. *Boom!* There it went. You ate all of the things you said you were fasting from. Your intentions were good, but you gave in to the temptation of the food.

Perhaps you made the commitment to go to church Sunday morning even after you went to the club Saturday night. You did so because "If I can club on Saturday, surely I can praise God on Sunday," right? So the club ends and of course, your homies or your girls want to stop at the Waffle House, IHOP or the Huddle House to get a bite to eat before heading home. So you probably don't leave there until around 3 a.m. You rush home to get some sleep before church. You're sleeping good, drooling, and snoring like it's nobody's business. Then the next thing you know, you look at the clock – it's 11:58 a.m. and church started at 11:00 a.m. *"Dang!"* is generally the initial response. Instead of going late, you just roll over and go back to sleep.

Maybe you can't relate to those examples. Perhaps you have a boyfriend or girlfriend or maybe you have a little "junt" you are kicking it with that turns into a "situationship" or "sinship." You have already decided you want to remain a virgin or to practice celibacy until marriage. You even communicated this to your significant other. But you started watching Netflix movies and chilling with the person. Of course, one thing led to another and the next thing you know, ya'll were having sex. Yep! You gave up the goods, and you probably were an emotional wreck afterward thinking about how you let yourself down and ultimately, how you let God down. Your initial desire was to refrain from any sexual activity but in the moment of passion, you were unable to stop yourself. The struggle was real – or was it?

## The Struggle is Real

Generally, we talk about the struggle being real when it comes to trying to get free from certain things or even in our efforts to complete tasks. *Merriam-Webster Dictionary* defines the word "struggle" as a strenuous or violent effort in the face of difficulties or opposition. It also means to proceed with difficulty or with great effort. After examining the definition, many of us can be honest and say that the fornication, gossip, promiscuity, masturbation, and pornography we engaged in were anything but a struggle. Yes! We may have contemplated not doing them, but we easily gave in to the temptation.

Maybe you were trying to find relief for your feelings of inadequacy, rejection, and abandonment. Or you just loved how powerful and in control sex and alcohol made you feel. But that one encounter turned from a mistake to a lifelong habit. It became an idol in your life taking up full residence in your heart, mind, and soul. It created a stronghold that caused you to backslide. Your faith, conviction, and pursuit of holiness suddenly vanished, along with your standards.

You can speak in tongues, dance, and have Baptist fits all day, but if they are not convicting or converting, you need to introspect. You need to check what kind of ghost you have because it might not be the Holy Ghost.

The evidence of temptation in one's life is not the problem or excuse because temptation is inevitable. No one is exempt from the presence of temptation. Even

Jesus Christ dealt with temptation in Matthew Chapter 4.

The Bible tells us that the Spirit led Jesus into the wilderness to be tempted by Satan. And after He fasted for 40 days and 40 nights, I'm sure His stomach was on empty, and He was hungry. This was a perfect opportunity for Satan because he gets his best results when Christians are weak. However, Jesus was not taking his bait and falling into the trap. Instead, He countered it with the Word of God as He remained obedient to God. After the enemy was unsuccessful, he departed, and the angels came to minister to Jesus.

As we can see, the temptation will come, but the temptation is not the sin. Sin only comes into play when we yield to temptation, which can sometimes be a gradual process until we are fully captured by it. But when we resist the Devil, deny access, and block all entrances into our lives, he has no choice but to flee.

> No temptation has overtaken you except what is common to mankind. And God is faithful; he will not let you be tempted beyond what you can bear. But when you are tempted he will also provide a way out so that you can endure it (1 Corinthians 10:13).

If Jesus could escape the tactics of the enemy, so can we. Do you think God is in heaven just waving temptation in our faces like a puppet on a string? No!

God is not trying to get you to sin, He is trying to get you to stay out of sin. That's the Devil's job all day and every day. He will use those things he knows you enjoy to try to reel you in.

God isn't going to make you live right or force Himself on anyone. He is a gentleman. Plus, from the beginning, we were given the freedom to choose. The Word of God gives us instructions. It is up to us to make the right choices and to live a lifestyle that is pleasing in God's sight. The Holy Spirit enables us to live accordingly.

When you start growing in your relationship with God, you will start loving what He loves and hating what He hates. Your desires will change, and you will no longer take the bait you used to fall for so easily.

Bait is used when fishing to lure the fish. The fisherman throws it into the water on a fishing pole. If the fish is hungry, they will bite the bait and get hooked. With that, the fisherman reels them in. However, if the fish is not hungry or interested in the bait, they keep it moving.

A lot of times, the Devil will only catch us because we are hungry for the very thing he puts in our faces. Which means you can't always blame it on the Devil. In actuality, you must take responsibility for your actions because you failed to kill the thought from inception.

That's why you must crucify your flesh daily! The flesh always wants to be satisfied – day and night. So crucifying your flesh is an ongoing process. Saying no to sinful desires is a day by day activity. Your decision to follow Jesus is far more important than one night of pleasure. Fleeing becomes difficult because the enemy will use various types of bait to entice us into traps that our flesh is longing for. Admit it. This flesh of ours is no good. Period. It is never satisfied. It never gets enough! That's why we find ourselves in a constant cycle of sin that must be broken. We have to kill the flesh daily by fasting, praying, and fleeing, while declaring we have the power over it and it doesn't have power over us.

> When tempted, no one should say, "God is tempting me." For God cannot be tempted by evil, nor does he tempt anyone (James1:13).

We all have desires and curiosities. The most many are taught at a young age is that we aren't supposed to do certain things. However, that's simply not enough in this day and time. Everything is overly sexualized, and temptations related to all addictions come from the north, south, east, and west. The most you preach to the people is "Don't do it." The Devil is a liar and a deceiver too. While we are saying "Don't do it," he is saying, "You don't know what you are missing." Superficial statements from the pulpit will not free anybody or stop people from experimenting.

When we were growing up, our parents would tell us not to do certain things. But they would never tell us why not to do it or how not to do it, especially when it came to sex. Not every parent gave detailed explanations about the "birds and the bees" because it was just something that wasn't talked about. It was just supposed to be understood.

Growing up, I was a very curious girl. If I was told not to do something without an explanation, the thought would constantly linger in my mind. I would question why I shouldn't do it. At times, I was curious and eager enough to find out – consequences and all.

I remember when I was in middle school; my mother was visiting my aunt and uncle in Virginia, which gave me enough time to be curious. She always told me that her contact lenses were off limits and I was like, "Okay, cool." Well, one particular night, as I was snooping in her bedroom closet looking for make-up, guess what I ran across – her contact lenses case. And you know what? The contacts were in there too.

I opened the case and inserted the contacts into my eyes. I was too excited. Of course, they were blurry, but they just seemed so cool. After a while, I was ready to take them out, but the jokers wouldn't budge. I was in big trouble. I even tried to cry them out but no luck. Have you ever tried to fit into a shirt that is way too small and then you couldn't get it off? That's how it was, and you know my reaction as well.

I jumped up and down, cried, screamed, and looked in the mirror every once in a while with the ugly face. Eventually, I had to call my aunt who came over and got them out for me. Whew! That was the last time I was curious for a while.

Remember, my mother had already told me not to touch her contact lenses. However, she failed to explain why. So I tried them out anyway. Before I did it, I went back and forth debating with myself whether I was going to put them in or not but eventually, a decision had to be made.

**Decisions. Decisions. Decisions**

Every day and throughout our lives, we have to make decisions, some major, others minor. What will I wear today? What will I eat? Who will I date? Who will I marry? What career will I choose? What car will I drive? The list goes on and on.

Accepting Jesus as your personal Lord and Savior is also a decision you made. I will applaud you because of all the decisions you made – that was the best of all. When you became a Christian, (I am sure that you probably realized sooner rather than later), your decision-making days were just beginning. Since then, you have fought a war. You have engaged in a fight within that demands a decision. That battle is between the flesh and the spirit.

**The War Within**

> So I say, let the Holy Spirit guide your lives. Then you won't be doing what your sinful nature craves. The sinful nature

wants to do evil, which is just the opposite of what the Spirit wants. And the Spirit gives us the desires that are the opposite of what the sinful nature desires. These two forces are constantly fighting each other, so you are not free to carry out your good intentions. When you are directed by the Spirit, you are under obligation to the law of Moses (Galatians 5:16-18 NLT).

Backsliding generally creeps in when you give in and decide to fulfill your personal desires and fleshly needs. Yes, there is a desire to live according to the Bible to please God, but our flesh and spirit are at war with each other. In Galatians 5:16, Apostle Paul tells us if we let the Holy Spirit lead and guide our lives, we won't fulfill what our sinful natures crave.

In our discussion about the flesh and the spirit, the flesh refers to our sinful nature. It speaks about the old man (or self). All of us were once spiritually dead because of man's fall in the garden of Eden in Genesis Chapter 3. Every human who was born after Adam and Eve has a sinful nature. Yes, we were born into sin, but we don't have to practice it. As a born-again believer, it doesn't have to be your lifestyle. We no longer have to fall victim to the sins we struggled with before becoming Children of God because of the sacrifice of Jesus Christ and His redemptive power.

If you are walking by the flesh, then you are not delighting in the things of God. Your pleasures come from the world. The desires your flesh produces are totally opposite to what is produced when you are walking by the Spirit. After the Holy Spirit opens our eyes to the sweetness of the gospel (John 16:8), and we become saved by grace through faith (Ephesians 2:8-9; Romans 10:9), we become new creatures in Christ.

2 Corinthians 5:17 gives us hope that if anyone is in Christ, He is a new creature. The old is gone, and the new is here. We are spiritually born-again, which means we have the ability and power to resist the evil desires of our sinful nature through the Holy Spirit. We have the ability to obey the holy desires of God, which are found in the Bible also through the Holy Spirit.

Without the Spirit, you are nothing but flesh. Paul said in Romans 7:18, "I know that in me, that is, in my flesh, dwells no good thing." Without the direction of the Holy Spirit, you are bound to make your own decisions. You will pursue what you want and your preferences, which more than likely are not centered on godly desires.

> The mind governed by the flesh is hostile to God; it does not submit to God's law, nor can it do so (Romans 8:7-8).

A mind set on the flesh demonstrates an unwillingness to be submissive to the authority of God. Whatever you give into you are submitted to. Think about it. Before you were saved, you would do what you wanted when you wanted. You made your decisions, not based on God's will for your life, but on your feelings, emotions, and intuition. All of your decisions may not have been bad, but even then, your choices were not solely based on consulting God or allowing the Holy Spirit to assist you.

In the world, choosing a boyfriend or girlfriend may have been less complicated than it is now. You made the decision based on your personal needs and where you were at the present moment. As a Christian, if you allow the Holy Spirit to lead you in your relationship goals, God will give you a new heart and put a new spirit in you (Ezekiel 36:26,27). Once this is done, His Spirit will dwell in you empowering you to walk in His ways and will.

No longer will you solely look at the physical appearances of a potential mate, but you will look deeper into their inner qualities and spiritual lives. Be certain they have accepted the gift of salvation and have a heart for God that will push you closer to God. Ensure your desire is not based on this point in your life but also on your destiny.

I didn't think about these things before I completely surrendered to God. My main interests were that the man I dated had plenty of money, a pretty smile, dope car, could make me smile and was tall enough for me to stand on my tippy toes to hug him. Listen, I'm just being honest. I admit my priorities were way off. Nevertheless, I began to grow into the woman God called me to be by reading the Word and applying it to my life. In doing so, I discovered who I was in God and what His desires were for me. Consequently, my desires for a mate changed.

I wanted more of what God wanted for me, and those spiritual desires became stronger than the fleshly desires I originally had. Fleshly desires? Yep! You know. Those sexual desires to sleep with that woman or man. Those urges to please them so you can feel "happy" and wanted. Be honest. All of us want to be loved and affirmed. We want to know someone other than our families and friends care for us just as much as we care for him or her. We usually look for this love and affection from a significant other.

Some of us will use any measure necessary to get someone to like us. Unfortunately, the things that are done are not always godly. Actually, we run the risk of "selling our souls" to get that sense of being wanted.

When I got baptized again in 2008, I was still in a relationship that I had been in for about two years. Although our relationship was going pretty good, it was still unhealthy. We were unequally yoked.

We did not have the same spiritual, future, or relationship goals. I knew this, and he did too. We constantly had arguments about these things and mostly, because I tried to make him be something he was not interested in at the time.

Ladies, you know how we are. We have this great ability to see the potential in our mates before they see it. Instead of being patient and helping them cultivate these things, we force our beliefs and our deadlines on them expecting them to change overnight.

This was a long-distance relationship. On Sunday mornings, I would call him bright and early to see if he was going to church. I would say things like, "You went to the club last night, are you going to church this morning?" Sometimes his response would be yes, and I would smile, but baby when that response was, "No, I'm tired"– that nagging queen came out. "What you mean you not going to church? God woke you up this morning and let you make it out the club alive and blah, blah, blah." I went "off off" like my niece Jaslyn says.

Just thinking about it now, I crack myself up because I can't believe this was actually me. I know I got on that man's nerves, but I promise it was from a good place. I just really wanted the best for him. Or did I want him to just be the best for me?

I wanted my man to be a reflection of me and in my mind, nagging would change him. Wrong! In fact, this is the very thing that pushes them away. Ladies, no matter how much we learned from our mothers or aunts about how to talk to a man, that doesn't mean it was right. No man wants to hear all that nagging and see all that neck rolling. Child, please! Ain't nobody got time for that. I learned a long time ago that you cannot change anyone. The person has to be ready to do that, and even then, it will take God, the Holy Spirit, and conviction to bring about transformation.

We mess up because we try to turn ministry assignments into mates. God called you to lead them to Jesus but you ended up leading them to your bed. You were so desperate and got excited just because they started talking about God and how much they wanted a closer relationship with Him. You used it as a perfect opportunity to develop that "perfect Christian relationship" you were praying about. You could just see it. You'll go to church together. Worship together. Read the Bible together and change the world together.

What you soon realize is that you spent so much time trying to lead the person to Jesus while dating him or her that you became stagnant and backslidden. You were drained of spiritual energy because you functioned in the wrong capacity. God did not call you to date the person but to disciple him or her. You should never have made it about you. As a matter of fact, it was never about you. It was all about God and helping the person develop a relationship with Him.

In this spiritual walk, it is vital that you recognize the importance of godly relationships and being equally yoked in all relationships from the get-go. You cannot continue to fall in love with potential. Repeat after me, "I am too valuable to settle. Point. Blank. Period."

Don't lower your standards or eliminate them completely just because you are tired of waiting or someone fails to appreciate your value. The more you entertain this, the more you will continue to fail in this area. Then you will have the nerve to ask why you attract all of the wrong people. You attract what you accept. If I accept and entertain guys hopping in my DM's and talk sexually to me, I shouldn't be surprised that all they want is sex. If you are a man who constantly hollas at half-naked females in the club with too little booty shorts on, don't be surprised when you only attract females who are loose and gold-diggers.

When your perspective and standards change, you accept that God wants what is best for you. You will no longer lower your standards or compromise. You will be drawn to those who already have a personal relationship with God.

Men, how can a woman have faith that you will effectively lead her in the future as your wife if you aren't even submitted to God's leading and guiding now? Do you have to be perfect? No! Does your relationship with God have to be like mine? Absolutely not, but I should have enough faith to know that when I am in despair or need someone to stand in agreement with the petition I have in front of the Lord, that I can trust you to cover me.

That's why discernment is crucial in relationships. Even the most anointed people will attract frauds just because of the gifts and anointing on their lives. A lot of people are attracted to the anointing and gifts, but not the spirit, mind, character or personality of a person. Discerning between the two is very important because your "now" connections can change the dynamics of your destiny. Your discernment can keep you from wasting unnecessary time with people who don't value what you value.

That's why it is important to be equally yoked, especially when it comes to saying no to the flesh. I can testify that it is super hard trying to live a sexually pure life when you and your mate are not on the same page.

**Let's Talk About Sex Baby**

First, let's get this out of the way: sexual desires are natural and God created us as sexual beings. That's a fact, not fiction. That being said, however, God made sex to be experienced between a man and woman who become one in holy matrimony. It's a beautiful thing to God when married couples are able to enjoy and celebrate sex with each other. Unfortunately, in our time, singles are having more sex than some married couples, and yes, that includes some single Christians. I used to be one of them.

I find it interesting that this topic is seldom addressed from the pulpits on Sundays these days. Nobody is talking about how to manage trying to live holy while you're still horny. I've not yet discovered the real reason why, but I would hazard a guess. The pastor is careful not to offend the praise team member, worship leader, musician, biggest tithe payer or even his or her private partner who is sexually active.

It reminds me of when I would push my toys under

my bed when my mother told me to clean my room before I could go outside. I would take a broom and shove everything I could under the bed. When she came to look at my room, she had little to fuss about, only what she could see on the surface.

Pushing the toys under the bed was a temporary fix. Eventually, I had to bring them out and tidy up before my mom inevitably found out what I was doing and I was exposed. It is the same with our sexual sins and addictions. If we don't deal with them and confront them from the root, eventually, they will get exposed.

We can't continue to sweep pre-marital sex amongst the saints under the rug. Instead, we must start calling it for what it is. This discussion needs to be had more often because it's one of the biggest things that continues to hinder believers.

**Celibacy**

If you were to conduct a poll on your Facebook page to see who is practicing celibacy, the number would probably be very slim because it's pretty much frowned upon by many. If you search the internet, you will find multiple definitions of abstinence and celibacy. Many times you will see it being used as one and the same, but there is a difference. If people are abstinent, they are merely just abstaining from sexual intercourse for whatever reason, not necessarily for a spiritual purpose.

According to Dictionary.com, celibacy is defined as

abstaining from sexual relations or marriage. For example, the priests in the Catholic Church take a vow of celibacy because they are not allowed to be married.

Others define celibacy as the act of abstaining from all sexual relations until marriage. I agree with this definition of celibacy to an extent only because I feel it is way more than just not having sex. If you limit it to just not having sex, you will miss the most important reason for it, which is an authentic commitment to Jesus Christ and the desire to please Him.

The definition of celibacy for a Christian should be abstaining from all sexual activities until marriage for a purpose and on purpose. The Bible is full of references which support the practice of celibacy and sexual purity.

In 1 Corinthians Chapter 7, the Apostle Paul gets straight to the point. "Now regarding the questions you asked in your letter. Yes, it is good to abstain from sexual relations. But because there is so much sexual immorality, each man should have his own wife, and each woman should have her own husband."

In vs. 3, Paul makes it very clear, "The husband should fulfill his wife's sexual needs, and the wife should fulfill her husband's needs." Now, remember Paul was single too, so he understood the temptations that many faced. In fact, if you read further into verse 8, Paul speaks specifically to the legally single.

Paul says that if you can't control yourselves, you

should go ahead and marry because it's better to marry than to burn with lust. Now, I know you may be saying, "Hold on!" You know good and well your relationship isn't that serious because you aren't ready to be anybody's husband or wife.

What if the law commanded you to marry the last person you had sex with? Oh! Your little heart may be crushed because even though the person was good enough to lay down and have sex with, he or she isn't good enough, in your opinion, to commit to. And unfortunately, many people have accepted this as the norm, which is why there is an increase of side chicks and secret sex buddies.

This is unacceptable, no matter how you look at it. Especially for a Christian. What surprises me is all of the side eyes and smirks I get when people hear I am practicing celibacy, and this is not even from the world but from the church. They look at me as if I made up a whole new doctrine about not having sex before marriage. Really? This isn't new. God has never been OK with premarital sex. His standard has always been holiness. Even in the times that I slipped up and messed up, it was still holiness. My lack of discipline didn't change it.

The problem is we have become so comfortable living in our dysfunction, we expect everybody else to be OK with it. Furthermore, we try to back it up with Scripture. The two most popular scriptures used to quote in self-defense are:

Do not judge, or you too will be judged. For in the same way you judge others, you will be judged, and with the measure you use, it will be measured to you (Matthew 7:1-2).

Let the one who has never sinned throw the first stone! (John 8:7).

These scriptures are usually quoted out of context. But the two sayings that put the icing on the cake for me are, "Only God can judge me" and "The Lord knows my heart."

I wish I could insert an emoji right here! Do you know the one with the eyes closed and the mouth straight? Or the emoji that is giving the stank side eye? Yep! Either of those would work perfectly fine.

In my pettiness, I always imagine a Zebra in Africa losing a stripe every time someone says, "The Lord knows my heart" in response to covering up sin or bad behavior. That saying runs me so low! I mean – really low.

When people say this, what they are really trying to say is that although they have sinned, their hearts are good enough to justify the sin. Actually, it's the very opposite.

No one sins because of a "good heart." Matthew 15:18-19 is very clear in saying, "What comes out of the mouth proceeds from the heart…out of the heart come evil thoughts, murder, adultery, sexual immorality, theft, false witness, slander."

Every action, whether good or bad, is a product of your heart. If you're rude to someone, cussing people out, being nice to people or even shacking up, guess what? All of those things just pretty much expose your heart and what you are or are not submitted to. If you are sinning, it's not because your heart is so good, but it's because something within has gone unchecked, and you need to get to the root of it.

Of course, you can say that only the Lord knows your heart because a man can't really examine inwardly. So you can hide the real condition of it from man, but you definitely can't hide your heart or lustful thoughts from God. Ask David.

David is someone we always look up to and model our lives after. The Bible tells us that he was a man after God's own heart (1 Samuel 13:14), but David had his flaws too, just like us.

If you read 2 Samuel Chapter 11, you see one day, David was walking around on the roof of his palace, and he noticed a beautiful woman bathing. He inquired about her. He learned her name was Bathsheba, the daughter of Eliam and the wife of Uriah the Hittite.

You would think the word "wife" would have made David go on about his business, not so. Instead, David operated in his flesh, allowed his lustful thoughts and flesh to get in the way and had sex with another man's wife. Not only did he have sex with this married woman, but David got her pregnant. (This is where you cue the song *"Confessions"* by Usher in your head).

This king after God's own heart committed adultery. To make matters worse, he had Bathsheba's husband killed and then married her. God was highly displeased with this, and David knew he had sinned, but of course, he tried to go on and live life as if nothing happened.

Eventually, David had to deal with the situation and wrote three psalms describing the months that he was out of fellowship with God (Psalm 32, 38 and 51). He tried to worship God but quickly found there was a barrier between them. In Psalm 38:6-8, David said, "I was bent over and greatly bowed down; I go mourning all day long. I am benumbed and badly crushed; I groan because of the agitation of my heart."

David truly loved God and felt guilty. He understood he had a heart problem and pleaded in Psalm 51:10, "Create in me a clean heart, O God; and renew a right spirit within me." David repented from the heart. He was truly sorry. I think that is what we are missing in the church today. People are no longer convicted when they do wrong, whether it sexual or not. Understand that sex is not the only sin we can commit. Fornication, uncleanness, lustful pleasures, idolatry, sorcery, hostility, strife, jealousy, outbursts of anger, selfish ambition, divisions, wild parties, envy, and drunkenness are just a few sins that are listed in Galatians Chapter 5.

When calling out sexual sins, some people are in denial that they are doing anything wrong. They figure if there is no penetration there is no fornication or adultery. Can I talk about it? You may not be going "all the way," but you are still having oral sex, anal sex, spending the night, taking vacations, and doing everything else that leads to sex. A lot of people are masturbating or watching pornography just so they won't add another "body" to their lists.

You are still committing sexual sin. Your thoughts are still not holy or pure when you are masturbating and watching pornography. You are pleasing yourself to relieve stress or to take that urge away. In any event, you are indulging in your fleshly desires. And until you get to the root of a thing, you can never fully be delivered from it.

One of the many reasons why a lot of Christians continue to fall in the area of sexual immorality day after day is because they don't recognize it for what it is. It is more than sex. It's spiritual warfare. It's a generational curse. It's a demonic spirit. It's soul ties.

The enemy wants to keep us bound. Therefore, he will tempt us, send distractions and use bait to reel us in so that he may keep us right where it is he wants us to be. The Devil is sneaky, conniving, and vicious. His main job according to John 10:10 is to steal, kill, and destroy us. Sad to say, Christians are falling right into his traps.

That's why the Bible tells us in 1 Peter 5:8 to "Be alert and of sober mind for your enemy the devil prowls around like a roaring lion, looking for someone to devour."

He wants to take us out. With this sin problem we have, we are pretty much making his job easier and easier. That battle is spiritual. Hence, we cannot keep trying to conquer fleshly struggles in the flesh; they can only be tackled in the spirit.

> For our struggle is not against flesh and blood, but against the rulers, against authorities, against the powers of this dark world and against the spiritual forces of evil in the heavenly realms (Ephesians 6:12).

If you have determined you can't be delivered from your sexual bondage, you are wrong. You can! Don't accept this as your reality and stop fighting. It does not have to be. Having said that, if we dig beneath the surface and unearth the truth, we will confess that some of us have stopped fighting because we love the pleasures of sin so much.

We know the moment we start fighting it and turning it down, we will be forced to give up the very thing we love. This includes food. You want that six-pack and slim waist, but your love and addiction to food during the hard times in life prevents it from happening. Be honest. You love having sex. You love the feeling it gives you and the zone that it puts you in while you are engaged in it, but after it is over, you still have to deal with the problems of your world – if not more.

**Consequences of Pre-marital Sex**

As much of a positive feeling sexual activity gives you, in reality, there are more negatives for the single Christian. That sin you keep toying with will cause you to forfeit your fellowship with God. You will find yourself running to the altar Sunday after Sunday. It will keep you from attending church because of your bothered conscience. You feel as if you're the only one dealing with it and everyone is judging you.

You will isolate yourself, which is exactly what the enemy wants. As pleasurable as sex is, it can lead to serious repercussions. Some people contract diseases they have to live with for the rest of their lives. Others have unwanted pregnancies. Some single mothers birth beautiful babies after having sex for the first time but have to deal with deadbeat daddies.

You may think masturbation is your private business, and it doesn't affect anybody – but it does – especially if you plan to get married. That selfish desire to please yourself will spill over to your marriage and if you are not careful, you will feel as if you can satisfy yourself more than your mate.

If you are sleeping with several women or men and you can't be faithful to your significant other now, what makes you think you will be faithful to your wife or husband? We are creatures of habit and those practices will follow us into our marriages if we fail to deal with them.

Single people are under immense pressure to get married. To many in the church, that's the solution to fornication and sexual immorality. But marriage doesn't get rid of the demons. If anything, it exposes them and makes your spouse vulnerable to them if not confronted.

If you aren't ready to marry a person and be in covenant with him or her, then you need to stop sexing the person. This is a serious matter. Don't let the desire to satisfy your sexual needs blind you to the destruction that person will have on your future. Of course, you may be able to "put it on them" like nobody else and make the person say your name, but don't be deceived. The ability to produce an orgasm neither equates to the need for a covenant nor is it an indication of love.

We wonder why it is hard to cut off those we have sexual affairs with even after ending the relationship and moving on. We also question why we have low self-esteem, depression, and homosexual tendencies. It is caused by the transfer of spirits from the people you bind yourself to sexually. Through sex, you have allowed those foul spirits to enter your soul, thus, creating soul ties.

A soul tie can be described as a connection between two people whose souls and spirits have been tied together through emotional, spiritual or, most commonly, physical association. Soul ties can be formed through close relationships, vows, commitments, promises, and sexual relationships. When you have spent time with someone and become vulnerable, a soul tie is bound to form.

It is important to understand that not all soul ties are unhealthy. There are healthy soul ties you can have with friends, cousins, and mentors. The Bible speaks of the soul tie between David and Jonathan in 1 Samuel 18:1 when it says that "The soul of Jonathan was knit with the soul of David, and Jonathan loved him as his own would." Jonathan was committed to the friendship with David and vice versa. There was nothing in this relationship that took the attention off of God or put each other in opposition to God and His ways.

If you engage in sexual intercourse with someone, whether married or not, a soul tie will be formed. Many souls are tied together because of vows and promises made: "I will never love anybody like I love you" or "No one will ever please me as you please me." Whether you knew it or not, you made a verbal soul tie to this person.

When your soul is tied, you will start picking up different attributes and characteristics from the other person. For instance, if you never struggled with pornography, cursing, clubbing, drinking, etc. it is possible you will adopt those practices even after the relationship is severed. You may also be surprised to know that spirits can be transferred from previous partners. Therefore, if you think because they are sleeping with that one person you are good and safe, you are mistaken. If the person you are sleeping with has had 20 partners, you have slept with them too. That's if that person has not divorced him or herself from the previous partners.

If not confronted, the same spirits that have been in their bloodline could easily attach themselves to you. Their demons have access to you because you opened that door. You may have detached from your partner, but it doesn't mean the person renounced or divorced his or her partners.

Yes, you may go to the health department and be free from sexually transmitted diseases. Condoms may be your physical protection, but they cannot protect you from soul ties. The more you refuse to deal with it, the longer you will suffer in silence or continue to backslide. I once heard a preacher say that "Sin will take you farther than you want to go, keep you longer than you want to stay and cost you more than you want to pay."

Have you counted the cost? Sin is costly! That's why I would rather practice celibacy than spend my life trying to break soul ties. I'm straight on that.

To get free from your soul ties, you must go

through a process of deliverance. It is the means through which someone is delivered from the bondage of an evil spirit or demon. Simply put, it is the casting out and expelling of demons in order to experience the love and freedom of Christ. At the same time, you are disarming the powers of darkness on your life. If you read the Bible, you will find many times when Jesus cast out demons. He also gave the disciples the power to do so as well. The same power, authority, and dominion Christ gave the disciples to cast out demons, He gave to us as believers.

> And these signs shall follow them that believe: IN MY NAME shall they cast out devils (Mark 16:17).

Demons are evil spirits that restrict believers' growth and advancement. This may be manifested in the form of affliction, temptation, accusation, and condemnation, to name a few. However, the most important thing to understand is they only have access when you give them an open door, entryway or legal rights to dwell in you. Demons are trespassers here on earth. They can only move and operate where people have given access. This access can be granted through sin, word curses, various life events, bloodlines, unforgiveness, and involvement with the occult, to name a few.

Below are some signs that indicate a person may need deliverance:

- False religions
- Addictions (drugs, nicotine, food, caffeine, medicine)
- Unclean sexual thoughts/acts (perversion, lust, homosexuality, fornication, masturbation)
- Emotional disturbance (jealousy, anger, resentment, rejection, fear)
- Mental torment
- Physical infirmity

The New Testament has many scriptures presenting evidence of the existence of demons. However, more importantly, it shows the power of Jesus in casting them out and providing freedom. This confirms that Jesus was and still is committed to rescuing His people from the kingdom of darkness.

Deliverance is essential to every believer, and it is our right to live in the freedom of God. However, deliverance is a decision and is ultimately for the decided. That means you will have to decide enough is enough. You must make up your mind not to let the powerless enemy have control over you.

Whether you are going through self-deliverance or deliverance administered by a minister, honesty is important. Be transparent about every problem area in your life for which you need relief to be more like Jesus. Demons love to use the weapon of secrecy against believers in hopes of blocking their desire for deliverance. Honesty announces to the enemy that you no longer desire to let him dwell in you, and you are in pursuit of freedom.

Not only is honesty required, but one must also be willing to confess, repent, renounce, and forgive. For this to work, you must come into agreement with God and the truth of His Word and break your agreement with every lie of the enemy. When you repent, you are literally turning in the opposite direction of the thing that had you bound and out of fellowship with God.

> If we confess our sins, he is faithful and just and will forgive us our sins and purify us from all unrighteousness (1 John 1:9).

You must be willing to accept forgiveness knowing that God is not like us humans who will pick and choose if we will bring the issue back up or not. God will show compassion and subdue your iniquities. Repent. Turn away from it. Return to God. He is standing there waiting for you with His arms open and ready to welcome you back home. The moment we identify our struggles, uncover and kill them is the moment we start our journey to freedom.

Years ago, my friends and I had a burn session. We met because we decided we wanted to experience the fullness of God in every area of our lives. Many of us were honest about things that were not dealt with or confronted from the past, especially our childhoods.

We decided to go into separate rooms and write down names, things, and places from our present, as well as our past that were keeping us in bondage. We included those we had yet to forgive. We wrote all of it down. We then read the list out loud, renounced everything on that list, and reversed every vow we made. This came with a lot of anger, tears, and release.

Once we were open and free about it all, we went into the backyard, put the lists in piles, burned them and told God to consume them. Once we swept our minds, hearts, and temples (houses) from the evil spirits, we prayed for Jesus to take residence inside of us. We asked Him to allow the fruit and gift of the Holy Spirit to fill those now empty spaces in our houses from which the enemy had just been stripped and removed. This was very important (Galatians 5:22-23, Acts 2:4).

> When the unclean spirit has gone out of a person, it passes through waterless places seeking rest, and finding none it says, 'I will return to my house from which I came.' And when it comes, it finds the house swept and put in order. Then it goes and brings seven other spirits eviler than itself, and they enter and dwell there. And the last state of that person is worse than the first (Luke 11:24-26).

If you don't fill your house, then it is left empty and

serves as an invitation to the enemy to return. It signals to him that nobody else is residing there, and he is welcome to return. The night we took action at our burn session was life-changing. I believe your deliverance and encounter with God will be nothing less.

If you haven't faced the reality of your truth and the things that have resulted in your bondage and mental prison, then it's time for you to do so. It's time for your deliverance. Any secret or evidence of your sin needs to be renounced and released. That includes abortions, miscarriages, STD, previous mates, childhood hurt, etc. Some people may even have soul ties to previous pastors, bosses, and leaders. You may still harbor feelings of resentment about how they did you wrong. Release it!

You may not remember everything verbatim, but just write down what you recall and renounce those things telling them they no longer have a hold on you. Don't be nice or try to reason with them. We don't counsel demons we cast them out. Let them know you reject any connection to them again. Deny, expel, and sever any hold. Bring it to its death. Have a funeral for it. Bury it.

Even after your deliverance session, there are things that you must do to maintain that freedom.

1. Maintain a consistent fellowship with God

2. Crucify your flesh daily

3. Develop a prayer life

4. Be committed to God

Also, you may have to be radical and rid yourself of everything tied to whatever it is that will make you relapse. That includes souvenir alcohol bottles, mattresses, jewelry, photos, gifts, clothes, and any other items. This may seem extreme, but the same intensity you had to get out of it, is the same fire and boldness you must have to stay out of it.

Be mindful that as you are getting delivered from a soul tie, the other person may feel the disconnection and want to reestablish the bond. This is not always the case. However, if it is, you should not go in that direction. Even if you have days of missing them, that doesn't mean you need to reconnect with them.

**Victory over Sin**

One thing I have learned about the enemy is that he will make you believe you will never overcome sexual sin. But as an ex-fornicator, ex-luster, and ex-porn addict, I found him to be a liar. God has given us the power and authority over the enemy. We have dominion over the tricks and schemes he uses to trap us. Believers are to dress in the full armor of God and stand our ground knowing we are not fighting for victory, but we are fighting from a place of victory.

You have control over your flesh to conquer the

power of sin. What you feed will grow! Therefore, you have to take authority over your flesh and crucify it daily. Tell it what to do, and it has no choice but to obey. Sometimes you have to starve it into submission with the very opposite of what it wants.

Inevitably, the enemy will bombard your mind with the mistakes, memories or failures of your past. He will make you feel you are not worthy enough to receive God's grace. Before you know it, you will be so condemned that backsliding seems to be the only option you have.

> There is therefore now no condemnation for those who are in Christ Jesus (Romans 8:1).

It is important to recognize there is a huge difference between condemnation and conviction. Conviction comes from the Holy Spirit, but condemnation comes from the Devil. Conviction should cause you to draw closer to God, while condemnation pushes you away from God.

> Salvation and the power and the kingdom of our God and the authority of his Christ have come, for the accuser of our brothers has been thrown down, who accuses them day and night before our God (Revelation 12:10).

The enemy will do whatever is necessary to drive a wedge between you and God by reminding you of how imperfect you are. Even if you are abstaining from sex or your addiction, he will make you feel as though you are no good. He will pressure you to throw all of those years and months of abstinence out the window. But you can't be deceived. God is not around here stuck on what you did wrong. Rather, He applauds your ability to get back up, shake the dust off, set your affections on Him, and keep it moving. The past should only be a place of reference, not your permanent residence.

By grace we are saved through faith and this is not from ourselves but a gift of God (Ephesians 2:8). The law of grace gives us the power to overcome sin, not the right to sin. It has nothing to do with our works. Grace gives you freedom without shame, guilt, or condemnation. You have been forgiven by the blood of Jesus and have the right to walk in your forgiveness.

> For freedom Christ has set us free; stand firm therefore, and do not submit again to a yoke of slavery (Galatians 5:1).

As a single trying to practice celibacy, it is going to take some work. Will it be easy at first? Probably not, but I can promise you that it will be worth it. Ridding ourselves of the familiar is a process. We know that familiarity breeds comfort. We like what is known to us and what ultimately feels good.

Deliverance is not for the weak or complacent. Reconditioning and retraining your mind requires commitment. The enemy will try his best to make you backslide because he understands your deliverance will help free others.

To live the celibate life successfully as God intended, you must stay in His presence. The more time you spend in His presence, the more He will fill the emptiness you may feel. You will begin to crave more of Him instead of that person, pornography or self-gratification. Your deliverance requires your participation.

**Set Boundaries**

Set boundaries in your relationships. For instance, you might want to eliminate kissing completely from the dating phase if you or your mate is easily aroused by a kiss. If you don't, kissing can eventually lead to sex.

**Avoid Spending Time Alone**

Avoid spending time alone at each other's houses, especially late at night. It might sound elementary, but sometimes it's necessary. Being alone in your house or apartment can make it difficult to resist the temptation to indulge and sexual activity. This also includes spending the night together. Don't put yourself in tempting positions that make you relapse.

**Have Someone Hold You Accountable**

Allow others to hold you accountable. This could be simply by telling them when you are planning a date night and sharing your whereabouts and when they should expect the date to be over. This allows not only for accountability but for necessary wisdom and guidance from those who are assigned to you.

**Be Modest**

Ladies, it is not smart for you to wear tight or revealing clothing. This can easily send the wrong message and also tempt the man of God who is trying to stay free from sexual sin. Fellas, this includes you too with your shirts off and revealing grey sweatpants. Help a Sista out!

**Fast**

Sometimes you have to fast from R&B music or other entertainment that takes your mind back to your past sexual relationships or keeps it in sex mode. Certain lyrics consume your mind and the next thing you know, you are playing those thoughts out in real life. The flesh is real.

When you have been delivered from something, it doesn't mean it has released its hold on you or will stop trying to pursue you. Prayer is a necessity, but prayer alone is not going to keep you from it. You will need to pray, flee, set boundaries, fast, be modest and accountable. The more you kill your flesh, the more you no longer embrace those desires. Setting boundaries, as well as having accountability partners you can be real with is essential. On days your thoughts and flesh are on fire it can go a long way in quenching your lust.

Make the choice to say yes to God and allow other people to understand later. You can't just want celibacy because your pastor said to do it or your friends are doing it; it has to be personal. It shouldn't be looked at as a punishment but as a joy. You save yourself for the one God intended you to marry while you are honoring God with every inch of you.

As you commit to the lifestyle of righteousness, you will start to experience the abundant life Jesus promised. Peace of mind will be yours. You will have joy in all areas of your life but most of all, self-control. You will need it. Whether you know it or not, sex can cloud your thoughts and in doing so, it can steal your joy and peace of mind.

Celibacy is actually pretty dope, especially when you and your mate are both practicing it. You will begin to develop a whole new perspective on dating/courting God's way. You will grow mentally, spiritually, and emotionally together without sex being the factor. It will force you to communicate without running to the bed for make-up sex. When married, sex will only be an added bonus to the relationship.

The kingdom of God is righteousness, peace, and joy in the Holy Ghost (Romans 14:17). This is your right as a believer. I speak that you will walk in your inheritance.

You can do it! And I declare guilt and shame will no longer be your portion. I dismantle every lie of the enemy and renounce every vow you spoke while you were in sin. I pray that fornication, lust, and perversion will no longer control your life. I pray that God will work on your heart and restore it from the inside out. May God send a godly mate your way when you are ready. As you wait, I pray that you will wait well and have the endurance to pursue Him like never before. I pray you will release the grip you have on the past because God cannot bless you with the new if you are unwilling to be detached from the old. I pray deliverance will be your portion and the deliverance minister will rise up in you to help others experience the power of deliverance and the joy of freedom.

## Spiritual Assessment

After reading this chapter, you may have been convicted about some areas of your life you have not submitted to God including your bondage to sexual sin.

If this is you, I want you to do as previously mentioned in the chapter. Write down every sexual partner, every childhood memory that still causes trauma, every addiction and so forth. Deal with them face-to-face. You may want to start with self-deliverance or reach out to the deliverance ministry at your local or a surrounding church to begin your process of deliverance.

**Recommended Deliverance Books**

*The Secrets of Deliverance* by Alexander Pagani

*Pigs in the Parlor: A Practical Guide to Deliverance* by Frank and Ida Mae Hammond

*The Finger of God* by Torace D. Solomon

*Deliverance and Spiritual Warfare* by John Eckhardt

*They Shall Expel Demons* by Derek Prince

The Spiritual Autopsy of a Backslider

# Chapter 6
# Faith on Trial

> Let us hold fast the confession of our hope without wavering, for He who promised is faithful (Psalm 139:23).

New Year. New Me. New Dreams. New Visions. New Faith.

This was the bold declaration I spoke loud and proud on December 31, 2015. I was determined that 2016 would be "The Year of the New" for me. I had an amazing feeling that God was about to take my faith to a new level. I was excited and on board.

My then pastor Bishop Kevin L. Adams, Sr. called a 16-day fast for the entire church in January, and I knew that I couldn't afford to be disobedient during this fast. I had some special requests before God including my career, finances, spiritual growth – and don't think I didn't insert a prayer for a new "boo thang." Yep! I sure did, and I was dead serious, but we will talk about that another time.

To make sure I succeeded in my fasting endeavors, I made certain my close friends and a few coworkers knew I was participating in the fast. They were amazing at holding me accountable while interceding on my behalf.

During the fast, I had a sense of expectation and hope that I hadn't experienced in a long time. I was so used to spending my time helping others fulfill their dreams that I became stagnant and complacent in some of the most important areas of my life. Of course, there is absolutely nothing wrong with making someone else's dream come true, but not to the extent of neglecting the dreams, visions, and plans God specifically gave to you.

As my sense of expectation continued to rise, I knew I had to put in the work. I had to sacrifice a few naps after work to make sure I completed at least five job applications a day and spent additional time towards my other goals. I was determined and my faith was at an all-time high. I even created a folder in my email for the rejection letters I received because I knew that sooner or later, an acceptance letter would come. And it did!

After two degrees and six years filled with denials, I finally landed a career as an Assistant Director of Athletic Communications in Intercollegiate Athletics. To say I was excited would be an understatement. I was overjoyed to know that God loved me so much He continued to watch over the Word concerning my life (Jeremiah 1:12).

Here I was, two months into 2016 and God had already blessed me with a new career in a new city and a new apartment. That was nobody but God showing Himself strong and mighty in my life.

Life was great. I quickly got acquainted with my new city, new job, and a new church. Most of all, I was finally able to see the benefits of my faith. However, if you know anything about life, no matter how much things seem consistent, the only thing in life you can count on being constant outside of God is change!

Just when you get settled and finally have your routine down packed, here comes life with its good self, changing up the game. And most of the time, it's not a small change. Nope! The change is usually big enough to knock the very breathe out of you. At least, that was the case for me.

Life for me changed drastically throughout 2016. Of course, it was good in the "honeymoon" stage. After the first few months were over, I found myself still trying to adjust to my new financial situation after taking a major pay cut in order to work in my field. It seemed like every other day for the first few months, I questioned if I had made the right decision.

I remember one person told me I needed to come back to my old job and city where I knew the money was good and where people were at. I definitely considered it, but deep down inside, I knew God had called me to this particular place for a reason; I just didn't know why.

As months continued to go by, I needed to hear from God concerning my situation quickly because my faith was slowly declining. Yes, you read it right! That faith I previously had, which surpassed the size of a mustard seed barely existed, and it just didn't make sense to me.

If I can be honest, I felt as if God set me up for the "Okie doke." My prayers, which were full of tears, probably sounded something like this, "God, how could you call me from a place of comfort into this place that has 'unstable' written all over it? You told me 2016 would be different, but how?"

Within one year, I went from blessing people through random acts of kindness, paying bills early, giving above my tithes and offerings, and being genuinely happy to not knowing what I was going to eat, deciding what bill was most important, getting a part-time job at McDonald's while having a master's degree, experiencing my first car repossession and slowly slipping into a depression.

My faith was on trial.

If you were to look up the definition of the word trial, you would find it is the process of trying to find the evidence of something. For instance, if you were put on trial in court, you would be examined before a judge or jury for the purpose of determining if you are guilty in a case, whether criminal or civil.

I believe that if many Christians' faith was put on trial today, the verdict would be guilty because a lot of people who say they have faith actually don't. See, when your faith is put on trial, it requires every part of you to be a witness on the stand including your patience, character, responses, etc. and if you are not careful, it will build or break you. Ask the three Hebrew Boys in Daniel Chapter 3.

The Bible tells us that King Nebuchadnezzar built a gold statue. Having done so, he commanded the satraps, prefects, governors, advisers, treasurers, magistrates and all the other provincial officials to bow down and worship the golden image whenever they heard the sound of the horn, flute, pipe and all other kinds of music. The king then made it clear that anyone who didn't fall down and worship would immediately be thrown into a blazing furnace.

Everyone obeyed the king's order except for the three Hebrew boys: Shadrach, Meshach, and Abednego. They loved God and were dedicated enough to only worship Him. It was personal for them.

Of course, just like that coworker who kisses up to management or the youngest sibling who always tells on the older sibling, a few men saw that the three Hebrew boys were disobeying the king's commandments, and they snitched.

King Nebuchadnezzar was furious! He called the boys to him and asked them if what he was hearing was true. If it was so, he promised to throw them into the furnace if they refused to bow. He also questioned what god would be able to rescue them.

Now, as a king, I am sure he probably thought that

confronting the three would cause them to retreat and obey him. However, my dudes clapped back like, "Bruh, we don't have to defend ourselves to you regarding this. Let's get something straight; even if you throw us into the blazing furnace, the God we serve will deliver us from it and from you. But don't get it twisted. Even if He decides not to deliver us, we still refuse to serve your gods or worship the image of gold you have set up."

I paraphrased their words, but you get the picture. They were *not* giving in! They had enough faith that God was going to deliver them from the fiery furnace and out of the king's hand.

If you continue to read, you will see that the king kept His word and threw them into the furnace. As the King peeped into the furnace, He was amazed because when they should have been instantly consumed, they were walking around in the furnace unhurt and unbothered.

Not only did he see the three, but he also saw a fourth person who looked like the Son of God in there with them. The only things that burned on them were the ropes that had them bound.

Nebuchadnezzar said, "Praise be to God of Shadrach, Meshach, and Abednego, who has sent his angel and rescued his servants! They trusted in him and defied the king's command and were willing to give up their lives rather than serve or worship any god except their own God" (Daniel 3:28).

The king was so astonished he called into the furnace and told them to come out. The officials gathered to see what the king was talking about, and they witnessed that not even a hair from the boys' heads was burned.

The Hebrew boys trusted in God and defied the king's command. They were willing to give up their lives rather than serve or worship any god except their God.

The king made a public announcement that anyone who spoke against the God of the three Hebrews would be cut into pieces and their houses turned into piles of rubble. The three were then promoted in the province of Babylon.

Talk about faith on trial!

Instead of them getting anxious and frightened by the threat of the king, these Hebrews decided to put their faith to work in one of the hottest situations they had probably experienced in their lives. Their faith was tried, tested, and proven to be true.

My grandfather, the great Reverend James Roberson once said, "A faith that can't be tested can't be trusted." As Christians, if there was ever a time we needed to have our faith tested to ensure we possess an unshakable, unmovable, mountain moving faith in God, it is now.

Contrary to popular belief, faith is critical in the life of a believer. In fact, it is one of the greatest assets we can have. If you don't possess faith in God during the most trying times of your life, it is an open door to backsliding as you try to make it on your own.

> Now faith is confidence in what we hope for and assurance about what we do not see (Hebrews 11:1).

In this particular scripture, Paul is showing us what our faith can produce when our hope is built on its firm foundation. The foundation of our faith is the Word of God.

> So faith comes from hearing, that is, hearing the Good News about Christ (Romans 10:17 NLT).

I am astonished at how many Christians claim they have faith, but they can't tell you much about what God has spoken in the Word of God or through His appointed messengers. This leads me to ask what is it you have faith in?

It is not enough to just say you have faith. Putting your "faith in faith" will produce absolutely nothing. The power doesn't lie in faith alone but in whom you put your faith. Your faith has to rest in God and the belief that He will do just what He said He will do.

> And without faith it is impossible to please God, because anyone who comes

to him must believe that he exists and that he rewards those who earnestly seek him (Hebrews 11:6).

Our goal should always be to please God in all we do. The harsh reality is that no matter how many church services I attend or how many good deeds I perform if I lack faith in God, I have not met my goal. Faith is a requirement, but it is invalid if the faith is not mixed with belief.

Unbelief is one of the biggest stumbling blocks in the lives of Christians. Truth be told, many of us believe Google more than we believe God because, in our minds, it makes more sense. Google gives us an easy way out. As a microwave generation, we typically want what we want and when we want it. The only problem with this is you will start placing your faith in the things that bring you instant gratification and relief in an effort to skip the process.

Misplaced faith is dangerous. Placing your trust in earthly things, including family, friends, and your feelings can be costly. Jesus is the Author and Finisher of our faith (Hebrews 12:2). He is well able to help our unbelief, as well as give us just what we need.

Many Christians backslide because they lack faith in God. This can happen for a number of reasons, but one of the main reasons is they feel God has let them experience things in life He could have gotten them out of sooner rather than later.

Maybe it's like a Mary and Martha experience in John Chapter 11. Their brother Lazarus was sick and Mary and Martha sent word to Jesus. Instead of performing an immediate miracle, Jesus sent word back saying, "The sickness is not unto death but for God's glory so that God's Son may be glorified through him."

Now if I was Mary and Martha, I would have said, "Jesus, thank you for that word, but can you speak a word and make him whole from where you are in Jerusalem? Because, according to John 1:1, 'In the beginning was the Word, and the Word was with God and the Word was God,' which means you, Jesus, are 'the Word.' Can't you just speak a word of healing?"

You would probably ask the same questions because generally, we all want to find a way to get out of the pain and disappointment that comes with some experiences. I'm sure these sisters were no different.

They probably were a little confused because Jesus loved Martha, Mary, and Lazarus. They had a genuine and strong devotion to Jesus. They were faithful to Him, and he identified them as beloved friends, but that didn't exempt them from going through what seemed to be a tragic and painful situation. Actually, they had to experience sorrow, sickness and then death because when Jesus found out that Lazarus was sick, He stayed in Jerusalem for two more days. When He finally arrived, Lazarus had died and already been in the tomb for four days. He stunk and his sisters were hurt and distraught. Wouldn't you be?

Jesus comforted them and Mary fell at his feet crying saying, "If you were here, my brother would have never died. How could you let this happen?" I could only imagine the pain she was in. She was faithful to Jesus and in her mind, the least He could have done was pull her brother through.

Maybe you have been where Mary was. You felt like you were faithful to God. You genuinely pursued Him with all of your heart, but you kept getting the short end of the stick. You lost your job while serving, lost a loved one while serving. Your body was plagued with sickness while serving. You went through a divorce and your child even went to jail all while serving. You were faithful to God, but it seemed as if your faithfulness yielded you nothing but trouble in the end.

Even Asaph in Psalm 73 felt this way. He was so fed up he started taking notes that compared his life to the life of a wicked man. He said, "The wicked have no struggles, their bodies are healthy and strong and they are free from the common human burdens." In verse 12, he said the wicked were carefree, but he explained how he remained faithful to God. Through all the afflictions, he even kept his heart pure.

He felt that good stuff kept happening to bad people and bad stuff kept happening to good people. The Message Bible says, "It's like a slap in the face." Asaph said this almost caused him to backslide.

This can be a very hard pill to swallow, especially if you have really tried to live this Christian life the best you can. You will even question if this thing is real or worth it. I have been there. When I was going through my transition in 2016 and my healing process after my broken engagement, I often times wondered if all of this was even worth it.

John the Baptist was God's appointed messenger. He was one who had uncompromising faith. He had that great honor of baptizing Jesus in Matthew Chapter 3. At that moment, the heaven opened and the Spirit of God descended like a dove.

In Matthew Chapter 11, John the Baptist was in prison, and he heard about all of the great things Jesus was doing. He sent his disciples to ask Jesus a simple question, "Are you the one or should we look for another?"

The question was delivered and Jesus told John's disciples to go back and tell Him, "The blind see; the lame walk; lepers are cleansed; the deaf hear; the dead are raised and the wretched of the earth learn that God is on their side."

John the Baptist was satisfied with this response. What he was saying is, "I don't mind going through what I'm going through as long as the glory is going to God. But I'm not interested in going through just for the sake of it. I need to know that this thing is real."

This is where a lot of Christians are today and

possibly even you. You're going through life, and you believe the Word of God. You have worked hard in the trenches; you have witnessed deliverance and people getting saved; you have laid hands on the sick and seen them recover. Then you come to a point in your life where everything that once was working for you is now working against you, and you find yourself questioning, is this thing for real?

The stories of Lazarus, Asaph, and John the Baptist let us know that even some of the most anointed women and men of God get discouraged, face afflictions, and are constantly attacked by the enemy, including our pastors and leaders.

This is why the church must do a better job in covering our leaders. It's just like football. A quarterback is usually sacked if he is tackled before he can throw a forward pass or if the offensive line isn't blocking for him when he gets tackled in the pocket.

Just like the quarterback, many of our leaders are taking unnecessary hits because too many Christians are more concerned about slaying their make-up and getting in formation for the beehive, than being intentional about slaying the enemy and getting in formation for the kingdom.

I have found that many believers have a misconception that as soon as they get saved, they should be free of any tests or trials and that the Christian walk is going to be the easiest walk ever. This thinking has continued to expose the real faith of believers because the first sign of a hangnail or situation, they are ready to walk out on it all.

They allow their emotions to be the driving force of most of their decisions, which typically leads them to be mad at the world but mostly God. They eventually walk out of the church all because of a misconstrued view that they should be living a life exempt from pain.

> Dear friends, don't be surprised at the fiery trials you are going through, as if something strange were happening to you. Instead, be very glad-for these trials make you partners with Christ in his suffering, so that you will have the wonderful joy of seeing his glory when it is revealed to all the world (1 Peter 4:12-13 NLT).

Peter is basically saying, "Don't get it twisted boo boo." He says you shouldn't even be surprised that you're going through the struggle of life. Is he discounting your situation? Absolutely not! But he is telling you your faith should be strong enough to look at the whole picture.

As a believer, even while going through, you should find hope in Romans 8:28, which assures us, "All things work together for the good of them who love God and to them who are called according to his purpose." In the midst of the trial and testing, it might not feel good, but trust it is working for your good.

Maybe you have tried to look at the bigger picture, but you find your faith slowly declining due to the constant hits you keep taking. Some faith in God is better than no faith at all.

In Matthew 17:20, Jesus told His disciples, "If you have faith as a mustard seed, you will say to this mountain, 'move from here to there', and it will be moved." Do you know the size of a mustard seed? It is super small. Jesus was basically saying, "I'm not even asking you for much faith but work the little you do have and watch it work for you."

That's why sometimes we need reality checks and to have our faith tested so we can be well-equipped to handle our situations "by faith." If not, your faith in God will waver, and you will find yourself trying to do it in your own strength. The trying of your faith is not to punish you but to prepare you.

In Psalm 73:16-17, Asaph had a paradigm shift when he had a reality check. In vs. 16, he said that it was all getting too much for him to handle until he went to church. Remember, from vs. 2-16, he was distressed, discouraged, and frustrated. On this Christian journey, you can testify that you have become exhausted, irritated, empty, and weak. If that's not your testimony, then I beg you to keep on living. But even in those times, it's not that you never had faith or strength, you just grew weary in your well-doing.

When you lose your faith in God, you can grow spiritually fatigued. This will lead you to stop fellowshipping with God and eventually, stop attending church. You will let your guard down and then the enemy will back you up in a corner and whoop you in your isolation. You will fall into his traps because you're fatigued.

Being fatigued, whether natural or spiritual is never good. If you are spiritually out of shape, the enemy will always gain an advantage because, in your weakness, you were ignorant of his devises. Although you may feel as if life isn't working in your favor or God is nowhere to be found, don't withdraw from church or God. In His presence, you will get answers, healing, revelation, and restoration.

Asaph had his doubts, and his faith began to fail him when it was up against the impossible. However, he went to church and received an "aha" moment. He began to get a new perspective on himself and then on the wicked. He was also able to face his reality.

Asaph knew he had no strength of his own and that he was weak, but he said in vs. 26, "God is the strength of my heart and my portion forever." That's the amazing thing about the God we serve. He will literally step in and hold us up when we are weak.

In 2 Corinthians 12, Paul had a thorn in his flesh and He asked God to take it away, which is what many of us do. Instead of enduring the process God is trying to take us through, we want to come out prematurely. Sometimes, God will say no, as He did to Paul, to fulfill what is necessary for your life.

Instead of removing the thorn from Paul's side, God said, "My grace is sufficient for you, for my power is made perfect in weakness." Paul said he would boast all the more gladly about his weaknesses, so that Christ's power may rest on him. He then went on to say, "For Christ's sake, I delight in weaknesses, in insults, in hardships, in persecutions, in difficulties. For when I am weak, then I am strong."

Feeling inadequate does not mean you are weak spiritually. It is just a perfect opportunity for God to show His strength and for Him to strengthen you. You have to let Him be your portion.

Yes, you may have mountaintop experiences and even seasons in the valley, but He is still God of both seasons. And even when the mountain is your blockage instead of your ladder, if you remember who your Master is, you will not have to be afraid of the mountain in front of you.

Whether it is exercising patience with your children or spouse, a hard time forgiving someone who has hurt you, starting a business or you just feel you can't make it another day, humble yourself and let God be all you need Him to be in that very moment.

He is a compassionate God. Lamentations 3:22-24 says, "Because of the Lord's great love we are not consumed, for his compassions never fail. They are new every morning; great is your faithfulness." God can be your portion if you allow Him.

You might be thinking of "portion" as a small amount. When I prep my meals on Sunday for the entire week, it requires portion control because it wouldn't make sense to have more than you need when trying to budget or lose weight.

I am very strategic with planning because whatever I cook on Sunday for the entire week will be my portion. I have to be sure it will still be fresh as a leftover. People always say, "How can you eat the same thing for five days?" as if they didn't grow up on leftovers. I got used to the portions, and they work for me. Using this system facilitated my weight loss and helped me budget successfully.

Think about this: God said He would be your portion in vs. 26, but would you be content with God alone as your portion? If He never blessed you again, would you be alright with that? If He never gave you the house, car, husband or wife you have been praying for, would you be satisfied with God as your portion? Is that a hard question for you to answer?

If we are honest, we wouldn't be quick to answer that because as much as we love God, we love the other things as well. Let me tell you the good news about having God as your portion.

Ladies, just like you go to the different weave spots

to get the bundle deals on the Brazilian and Indian hair, God also has a package deal. In fact, He is the package deal, which means even when it seems as if you are losing, you are actually winning. When God is your portion, you have access to everything He is and everything you need Him to be. Having God brings joy, peace, a renewed mind, love, eternal life and so much more.

## Growing Pains

Of course, it doesn't take away from the constant battles you may have to face or the fact that trouble seems to always find you. However, you can rest assured that while you're facing your various trials, you are growing.

It doesn't feel good. Of course not, but you can't allow your circumstances to dictate God's goodness. Even in the discomfort, He is still good. The truth of who He is doesn't change. He is the same yesterday, today, and forevermore.

Even when you were a child, and you felt like your bones and muscles were hurting, your parents would say, "Aww, hush up! It's just growing pains." It doesn't feel good at the moment, but you will appreciate the growth later on down the road.

Trying to trust God in your transition to a new city becoming an entrepreneur, applying for a new job, learning to do life without someone you thought would always be there will entail some pain and discomfort.

When you accept the growing process for what it is, you allow God the opportunity to shape and mold you – not some of you but all of you. He will start changing your attitude, mindset, and inability to forgive or to love without reciprocation. He will shine a light on all of the places you've failed to deal with along the way.

It does not feel comfortable, but God is more concerned about your character than He is about your comfort. Look at the children of Israel. They were in the desert for 40 years because they failed to go and grow through the process as intended.

Instead of following the instructions of their leader, they decided to murmur and complain. God made them a promise to deliver them from Egypt and take them to the Promised Land. But He had to make sure they were ready for what He wanted to bless them with.

God knows if He gives us what He promised us or what we pray for before we are ready for it, we could mishandle the blessing.

Maybe you are like the children of Israel. You feel you have been wandering in the wilderness for too long, and your faith is nonexistent. Hear me out. Could it possibly be you still haven't learned the lesson God tried to teach you years ago? Is that why you are still in the same spot? Is that why you are going in circles and cycles?

You are asking God to give you new instructions when you haven't obeyed the last set of instructions you were given.

It's not that God doesn't want to deliver you and bring relief to your situation. He just needs to make sure He can trust you with the next level. You have to learn how to master the process, not rush it. You can't get fresh collard greens in a microwave or in 20 minutes. I tried it, and it doesn't quite work like that. Those things came out of there tasting like pure grass, but you better believe that I eventually mastered it. And if I didn't learn anything else, I learned quickly that good things take time to simmer.

## GPS (God's Purpose Served)

Just like the Israelites had to take a long way around, sometimes God will require that we do the same for His purpose to be fulfilled.

I remember when I first got the iPhone 6 in 2015. I was so excited. A few days after I received my phone, notifications continued to pop up on my screen requesting to update the software that Apple provides. I had already ignored the request a few times and decided on Friday night I would complete it.

The following Saturday after I successfully updated my phone, I jumped into my car to head to Saturday church, and Siri started talking. The first thing she said was "15 minutes to Chattanooga." I was a little thrown off because I had never heard her say that before, but I just continued to drive off.

As I was approaching the stop sign, I heard Siri say, "Turn left." At this point, I was all the way confused because although I didn't insert an address into the GPS (Global Positioning System) on my phone, Siri was giving me accurate directions.

I decided to pull up the GPS and lo and behold, my church's address was in there. My eyes bucked so fast because I knew the directions to my church's address by heart. I was there four to five times during the week and every single Saturday.

Later, I realized Apple's technology had become smart enough to keep track of your familiar destinations, routes, and time; it automatically stored the information on your phone.

Before I could begin to research it, God immediately revealed to me that just like the GPS knows where I'm trying to get to without my assistance, so does He. He is trying to orchestrate our lives to reach a particular destination but instead of listening to Him, we remain lost or continue to wander around.

Instead of taking heed to Proverbs 3:5, we do what we want and end up at dead ends. We get lost along the way. How crazy is it that we trust a GPS, which is manmade, more than we trust God, the maker of man?

My GPS fails me daily. When I was in New Orleans

for the Full Gospel Baptist Church convention, I was never that lost in my life. The sad part is I was using the GPS. The problem was that the GPS didn't pick up the fact that construction was being done in certain areas causing detours.

God knows all about life's detours, unlike the GPS. God knows the bumps, bruises, and potholes we will experience before they happen. Because we won't have trust issues with God, we would rather pick up baggage along the way or create our own delays.

> The Lord directs the steps of the godly. He delights in every detail of their lives (Psalm 37:23 NLT).

The way God is directing you may not be what you would have chosen for yourself, still, trust the fact that He is God, and He has your best interest in mind.

Will there be some delays? Probably. Will there be some detours? I'm pretty sure, but a delay or detour does not necessarily mean a denial. It might just mean God is protecting you or processing you to be better equipped before your delivery or arrival.

We say church clichés like, "While you're trying to figure it out, God has already worked it out." I love the end part of that phrase, which lets us know God has already worked it out. However, the beginning part is what gets a lot of us in trouble. It was never intended for us to figure out God's plans. We are just supposed to trust them. What is faith if you must always know every minute detail before you make a move? What is faith if you are more dependent on your own logic?

For we live by faith, not by sight (2 Corinthians 5:7).

The need to know all the details just exposes the fact that many are control-freaks and have to be in control at all times. Faith will require you to dismantle all doubt and take a step into the unknown without knowing the full plan.

Walk by faith, not your feelings. Walk by faith, not opinions. Walk by faith, not your comfort. Walk by faith, not your understanding.

We love to recite that the steps of a good man are ordered by the Lord, but how can God order our steps if we never take them? Many times, when we say that we are waiting on God, the truth is that He is waiting for us to make a move. Once you make that first step, you will find that you were stressed or worried for no reason.

> The Lord will work out his plans for my life-you're your faithful love, O Lord, endures forever. Don't abandon me, for you made me (Psalm 138:8).

To others, the year 2016 probably looked like the worst year ever for me and at the time, it felt like it. I literally thought God had failed me. However, it turned out to be one of the most beautiful experiences of my life. The pieces of the puzzle started coming together one by one and at the end of 2016, I learned it was all necessary.

Yes! My car was repossessed but within 15 minutes, someone sowed that money into me to pay the bill and retrieve my car. Yes! I had to work two jobs at the time, but I went from flipping burgers to obtaining a better second job that would assist me in paying off debt.

At the end of 2017, I was promoted and became the first woman Director of Athletic Communications at the historically black college where I was employed. I started to develop the gifts of the Spirit while growing as a preacher, deliverance minister, and intercessor. My faith was shaken, but it was restored. Every tear and disappointment, all the embarrassment and the setbacks were worth it. I was put up against the fire and I had no choice but to trust God with everything concerning me. He literally became my provider, way maker, strong tower, great deliverer, joy, restorer, and most of all, my "good, good Father."

I didn't understand it then and if He would have told me what I had to go through to get to the place I am in now, I probably would have said, "Naw, I'm straight." But He changed my perspective, and it changed my life.

If I was told to describe the year 2016 in two words, I would still stick with the "new" concept, but I would add "oil" to it.

New Oil.

See, my 2016 was similar to the fried bacon experience. Bacon is one of the only meats you can fry without having to add oil. When bacon is put up against the heat, it produces its own oil. 2016 produced a new oil for me. Just like an olive, I went through the shaking, beating, and pressing, but the anointing that rests upon my life is stronger than ever before. I am better because of it.

If you learn to trust God in your process, you wouldn't allow your faith to decline so drastically that it sends you into a backslidden place.

Everything God does is good, and He wants what is best for you. It might be tough. You might even have to encourage yourself, but God is only preparing you for better. Some trials are necessary. God will not take you from the frying pan to the furnace unless He has equipped you.

You are more qualified than you think.

Many of us are frustrated because God is calling us to create something that we haven't seen yet and that we don't have a blueprint to refer to. This can be scary and intimidating.

One of the hardest seasons to be in is a season when God appears not to be speaking to you when you feel He is silent with no instructions or directions. It is in the quietest seasons that you have the opportunity to draw closer to God. Don't retreat believing His silence automatically means no.

If we make that assumption, it can weaken our faith because we feel we are not capable of doing the task. In fact, that imposter syndrome will come upon us, and we will feel we are fraudulent. We don't realize many of the people we look up to on social media have had failures; they just show us the highlight reels. But if they opened up their lives, you will see they made some mistakes from time to time. Nevertheless, they learned how to fail forward and not quit whether they had all of the answers or not.

You can't continue to let your lack of faith or sheets of questions keep you stagnant or out of sync with God. God is always progressing and moving and He will frustrate your comfort zone enough to push you out of stagnation into the place He needs you to go.

He isn't trying to stress you, He's trying to stretch you.

Of course, it will be like Peter walking on water for the first time. A lot of people like to criticize Peter because he started to sink when he took his eyes off of Jesus. But even though he started to sink, I can applaud the fact that he didn't go under, while recognizing the courage it took to get out of the boat.

People will have their opinions when it comes to you taking risks, but don't spend time listening to criticism from people who are still in the boat.

I'm sure Peter was uncomfortable taking the first step out of the boat, but the most success comes outside of your comfort zone and the limitations you set on yourself.

For your faith to increase in this area, you need to divorce your plan and personal blueprints, while leaving your comfort zone. Truth be told, the comfort zone only gives you the excuse to be a coward and a person who stays in the box because of the fear of success or failure.

Your job is not to know all of the answers before you start it, buy it or obtain it. If it is God's vision, you must have faith enough that He will provide the provision, resources, clients, and partners. He will take you to the greatest extreme where you can see the promise, but it is the farthest thing from the word that was spoken. This is when you have to work the middle. This is where you must allow God to stretch you in your area of faith understanding your response in the middle of a thing determines how mature you are and how much you have grown or need to grow.

As you trust God even when you can't trace Him, He will know you can be trusted with a little more at a time. He will begin to download strategies, wisdom, understanding, and clarity regarding every path, plan, and vision.

Many of our plans are not working because we haven't had faith enough to submit them to God. The moment you realize you don't know all of the answers is when God can give you just what you need. James 1:5 tells us that if we need wisdom, we can ask God and He will give it to us generously. However, you can't be afraid of your own success, no matter how many times you failed. Fear of failure, success, resources or lack of support should never be part of a believer's life.

Fear is the opposite of faith, which means it comes from the enemy. God has given us power over fear. You can't be fearful and faithful at the same time. You have to decide which one you are going to walk in. You must starve your fears to feed your faith. When you decide to look at your circumstances through the eyes of God instead of the eyes of your circumstances and limited understanding, you will find rest in the fact that God can do anything but fail. Declare, "There is no quit in my blood! I will endure until I cross the finish line."

Trust the process and allow your faith to overshadow the fear of the unknown. You don't have to be in competition with anyone else or compare yourself to other people's timelines. It's a journey, not a race. Free yourself from false expectations and burdens. It's your race, at your pace, in your lane! Let the Holy Spirit lead and guide you concerning the speed limit and exits to get on and off.

God may make you wait but just imagine how pleased you will be when you see the results of the wait. I don't know about you, but I believe every no or not yet is a blessing in disguise. I believe He is going to blow the mind of the waiter due to obedience.

> However, as it is written: "What no eye has seen, what no ear has heard, and what no human mind has conceived"- the things God has prepared for those who love him (1 Corinthians 2:9).

My prayer is that you would increase your faith and trust God in every area of your life. I speak that you will no longer be timid or hesitate in asking God for what you have faith for and that the season of "ask and receive" is upon you. I declare that your level of expectation will birth a divine manifestation. I speak that you will no longer try to handle things out of your own intellect, timing, or will, but that you would trust God's timing as it concerns your life and future. I speak peace to every area that screams anxiousness, doubt, and fear and I declare that you have authority and dominion over them. I declare and decree that your plans are submitted to God and that you are right where He wants you to be. And in the name of Jesus, I decree and declare that you will have unwavering mountain moving, storm destroying and water walking faith that shall not be shaken.

## **Spiritual Assessment**

Think about every area of your life in which you have failed on your faith walk and in your inability to trust God. Write down those areas: relationships, marriages, businesses, the future, your children, healing, deliverance, ministry, etc. Write down how you will turn those areas into places where you can build your faith in God.

The Spiritual Autopsy of a Backslider

# Chapter 7
# Pray It Through

Never stop praying (1 Thessalonians 5:17 NLT).

When I was growing up, I loved Sunday school and Bible study. I loved to read and learn new things. In Sunday school, I recall each class taking up the offering. As we put our money into the offering plate, our Sunday school teacher would make us release it with Scripture. Of course, she eventually had to put a stop to the use of "Jesus wept" as the offering scripture because we wore it out; it is the shortest verse in the Bible.

Before we went upstairs with the offering, someone had to pray over it, and I ran every time. I would look down and close my eyes super tight, so she would think I was tapped in.

I was terrified of praying. Our church was filled with prayer warriors, and I felt like my prayers were below preschool level. As I got older, I remember during Bible study, they would allow someone from the youth department to open up in prayer before dismissing for individual classes. I jumped up for that one because the easy way out was just to have everyone bow their heads and repeat the Lord's Prayer together. I had that one in the bag.

As I grew older, of course, they needed the Lord's Prayer to be retired as the opening prayer; they wanted a legit prayer. So what did I do? I came late to Bible study or waited outside like some of you do until you know you are in the clear. I know it sounds ridiculous, but it was the fear of saying the wrong thing or not saying enough that had me bound.

I look back now, and I honestly don't know why I was even fearful because my church was very loving. Not only did they teach us how to pray, but they would also encourage us while praying.

In high school, I started praying a little more but only when I needed something or when I felt like I was in despair. I would pray for God to let me pass a big test whether I studied for it or not. I would pray that I make the cheerleading squad or that my mom or dad would say yes to the money I was asking for. I had selfish motives and treated God as if He was a genie in the bottle.

Then came college and things started to get real.

Life started happening and before I knew it, I had a full-blown prayer life. I started experiencing trials, heartaches, failed friendships, and bills that required me to spend more time in prayer with God. At one point, it was as if God disconnected me from the world just to get me to be alone with Him. It hurt, but it helped.

That's how it usually happens. We live as we please and when we encounter life-altering experiences or at the end of broken dreams, we are down-spirited, lose hope, and fall at God's feet in desperation.

We cry out to Him as hard as we can and usually make up lies like, "God, if you let me get through this, I promise I will start going to church." God answers our prayers in some form or another and we put Him back on the shelf until we need Him again. After we get what we want, we are satisfied enough to tuck Him into that place which says, "for emergency use only." And Lord forbid you don't get what you want. You become frustrated, and you blame God for not coming through for you when you "needed Him most." Consequently, you turn your back on Him and the church completely, but only because you had a misconstrued view of prayer in the first place.

It amazes me that people will pray one prayer and if God doesn't answer them in the way or timing they expect Him to, they give up. If Jesus had to pray three times in Matthew 26:36-46, what gives you the right to think your one short prayer should be enough?

I love the parable of the persistent widow in Luke 18. She relentlessly asked the judge to give her justice in her situation. She refused to stop until she got what she wanted. She was persistent. Jesus honors persistence, not just protocol. He honored the prostitute who crashed the party at the Pharisee's home to anoint his feet. He healed the woman who pressed her way into the crowd to touch the hem of His garment.

When you really want something, you will

continue to request it for as long as you need to until God answers. There are some things that you will have to tarry and war for in prayer. The effectiveness of one who prays is not in how cute the prayers are or how well the subject and verb agree but the inability to keep praying until they get a breakthrough and ultimately an answer.

However, if you don't understand the purpose of prayer, you will always pray amiss without tapping into the will of God concerning the situation. Viewing prayer as a mere way to get what we want from God brings about disappointment every time. Prayer was never intended to be a list of wants and needs that we bring to the Father for our own sake.

Think about what you have prayed for over the last month. What does your list look like? Is it spirit led or filled with fleshly desires? If you are honest, it is probably all about what you wanted with a bunch of demands.

**The Purpose of Prayer**

Prayer is a dialogue between God and His children. Prayer is essential to the life of every believer and just as oxygen is needed in the physical, prayer is needed in the spiritual. As a Christian, there is no way for us to be effective without it. Just like a relationship needs communication, our relationship with our heavenly Father requires communication as well.

Prayer gives us the opportunity to have one-on-one communication with God. When it comes to making decisions, needing clarity, and seeking healing, God provides all of this and more in prayer. The Bible confirms in 1 John 5:15 that God hears our prayers: "We know that he hears us in whatever we ask, we know that we have the requests that we have asked of him." However, in any relationship, it is never fun when only one person is doing all of the talking and fails to listen to anything the other person is saying. That is what a lot of us do in our relationship with God.

We go to God with a bunch of demands, complaints, and frustrations. Once we finish dumping all of this at His feet, we proceed to get up and leave our places of prayer. How rude! It reminds me of when you call people for something, but before you can get your request or concern out, they have already dumped theirs on you. At that point, you forget what you were going to say or you just decide to forget it.

Prayer is a two-way street. God has a response to everything that concerns us. If we sit still long enough, the Bible promises that in our seek and pursuit of God, we will find Him and He will speak to us.

> You will seek me and find me when you seek me with all your heart (Jeremiah 29:13).

Praying with the power inside of you can cause

situations to change quicker than you can imagine. It can cause giant-sized problems to become small when the anointing is attached to it. When you pray, you minimize the problem and maximize your God.

That's why you can't continue with the excuses.

Let me guess, your schedule is super busy? You have to get your kids ready in the morning, meetings all day at work, and then have to get your family together at night just to turn around and do it all over again the next day. I get it.

For some reason, we have looked at "busyness" as something that validates us. Just because your schedule is filled with church activities, doesn't make your busy schedule an acceptable excuse not to pray. And to be honest, many people are busy but not productive, so the least you can do is include time for prayer.

God never intended for you to crowd your calendar so much that it takes you out of His presence. At some point, you have to recognize you can't afford not to pray and spend time in His presence.

The devil walks around the earth to and fro looking for whom he can devour. He doesn't rest, so I am wondering why you think it is OK for you to come off your post. You have a full-time enemy with a part-time prayer life, and you wonder why you keep losing battles.

The enemy knows there is power in your prayers,

especially when you are interceding for someone else. Don't use the excuse that you don't know what to say like I did. God is not looking for a super long, drawn out prayer. He is not looking for eloquent words. He just wants a sincere lifestyle and a pure heart that seeks Him.

Sometimes you will have to turn your plate down just for the sake of fasting. Jesus fasted 40 days and 40 nights in the wilderness in order to die to His flesh and hear from God concerning His future. You will have to do the same sometimes.

It might be hard saying no to that donut, Big Mac or even social media, but the more you turn down what you want for what God wants for you, the easier it will become. You will eventually turn it into a lifestyle.

**The Power of Prayer**

Prayer is important because Jesus encouraged us to pray in Matthew 6:5 and Luke 18:1. However, it is also necessary because it keeps us dependent upon Him while reminding us that His ways are higher than ours.

Prayer keeps us humble and sensitive to the voice of God and the directions of the Holy Spirit. When we pray, we are strengthened for our journeys while having strategies to gain victory over the enemy. Often times when we have neglected our time in prayer, we lose our focus, but prayer will immediately redirect our focus on the purpose and will of God.

According to Scripture, we pray to the Father in the name of Jesus through the power and with the help of the Holy Spirit.

**Model of Prayer**

You might be at a place where you don't want your prayerlessness to keep you out of fellowship with God. He wants to see us succeed on the Christian walk, and we should want to as well. If we are going to do so, prayer must be a lifestyle for us to stay in constant communication with God.

When I started praying, I journaled to God and wrote down my prayers. I would read my Bible during every quiet time, and I made sure I was prepared when I went into my tranquil space.

One thing that helped me stay focused in prayer was using the following acronym:

**P - Praise and Thanksgiving –** Giving thanks and praise to our Lord and Savior by worshiping Him for who He is and thanking Him for all He has done. Also reverencing Him and making His name great above all other things.

**R - Repentance –** Asking for forgiveness in all areas of your life (thoughts, attitudes, sins, unmanaged time, etc.) This ensures there is nothing blocking or hindering clear communication between you and the savior.

**A – Asking for Others –** This is a time to intercede for others, as well as the nation. If someone asked you to pray for him or God put it on your heart to pray for someone specifically, make a list and take it with you in your prayer time. Doing so allows you to be very intentional about touching and agreeing on the person's behalf.

**Y- Yourself –** Now is the time to pray for yourself and pour out the sentiments of your heart about what you want God to touch in your life. Many times, we find it easy to pray for others, but difficult to pray for ourselves. Either we feel we don't deserve what we are praying for or we feel selfish. Trust me, you deserve it and you are not selfish to petition the throne on your own behalf.

When I journal to God, I always go back months later to read what I was praying for in that particular season. I am always blown away by my prayer requests and to see that God answered them or exceeded my expectations.

**Praying the Word of God**

Another thing I learned to do that has changed my spiritual life is praying the scriptures. When I had no words to say and didn't know what to pray, I looked up scriptures concerning my situation (financial, healing, depression or etc.), and I just repeated them to the Lord. For example:

"Lord, you said in Philippians 4:19 you will supply

all of my needs according to your riches in Jesus Christ."

"Lord, your Word says in Isaiah 53:5, you were wounded for our transgression; you were bruised for our iniquities; the chastisement of our peace was upon you and by your stripes we are healed."

Prayer mixed with the Word of God is one of the most powerful spiritual tools any believer could and should have. Both are lifelines for believers.

> God's word is an indispensable weapon. In the same way, prayer is essential in this ongoing warfare. Pray hard and long (Ephesians 6:17-18 MSG).

The Bible tells us that God's Word, when spoken, will not return void but will accomplish its purposes on the earth (Isaiah 55:11). When we pray the Word of God, we can be sure it is secure and a firm foundation that will produce results. His promises are "yes and amen." When we pray the Word of God, we can approach it with confidence knowing we are not praying out of our will, emotions, or feelings. Rather, we are praying what He has said.

> This is the confidence we have in approaching God: that if we ask anything according to his will, he hears us (1 John 5:14)

This means that if we aren't seeing results or

answers after we come out of a place of prayer, it may because it isn't His will. And if it's outside of His will then it is also off of His radar in the realm of prayer. There is no reason believers should be questioning what the will of God is because we can find it in the Word.

> If you abide in Me, and My words abide in you, you will ask what you desire, and it shall be done for you (John 15:7).

When you find it hard to concentrate in prayer or find the words to say, it is generally an indication that your Word intake is not where it needs to be. The Word of God is nourishment that trains, teaches, and sustains. It is to be used as a weapon against the enemy. We need the Word of God and as long as we find ourselves in the Word, the Word will find itself in us.

When you don't know what to pray, start praying the scriptures over your life. Not only will your Word intake increase but so will your ability to pray effectively.

## Hearing the Voice of God

Many people get confused and discouraged in prayer because they are waiting to hear God in an audible voice, and it hasn't happened yet. God can speak to us in many ways including through a still small voice, thoughts, dreams, visions, the Word, an audible voice, nature, prophetic art, and through others.

Often times, you may be looking for Him in the thunder, but this may not be the case for many of us. First, you have to position yourself to hear from God. You must also remove all distractions, as well as quiet your soul and mind. Invoke His presence into your space through praise, worship, and by reverence. Ask Him to speak to you and expect Him to respond. Samuel said, "Speak Lord, for I, your servant, am listening."

Then here comes the fun part. Wait. That's right. Wait in silence for God to speak and answer you. Wait until you get a revelation from God. You can even take a pen and paper into your quiet time with you to write down what you hear or see. It might be words, images or thoughts. Write what you hear without overthinking. Later, test the word by making sure it lines up with the Word of God and the truths of God.

If you want to be keen on hearing God, having devotions with Him is necessary. Pursue and commune with Him to learn His character, nature and most importantly, His voice. Jesus says in John 10:27, "My sheep hear my voice, and I know them and they follow me." Learn to discern the voice of God just like children know the voices of their parents whether they are in a room with two or hundreds.

As you spend more time with God, you will become a skilled listener and recognize Him in everything. You will receive revelation through prayer to make sure you are in alignment with His will. Prayer doesn't have to be hard. Invite God to give you revelation by asking what He is saying about a particular subject.

God, what are your thoughts on this school I'm applying to? God, what is your opinion on this person I am interested in? God, what are your instructions on my next career change?

God has something to say and you will have to put all fear, doubt, and unbelief to the side regarding your ability to decipher His voice against your own.

## Different Types of Prayer

There are many different types of prayers believers have access to and can use no matter the situation or need.

**Prayer of Worship** - This prayer is focused on reverencing God and adoring Him. We don't focus on asking Him for anything but simply on praising Him for who He is and becoming one with Him.

In Luke 18:35, Jesus is met by a blind beggar who cries out for help. And after Jesus has a conversation with the man, He heals the man and restores sight to his eyes. The man walked around glorifying God. When the people saw it, they didn't ask for anything; they simply gave praise to God.

**Prayer of Petition** - This prayer is between you and God when you are asking for a particular request or a specific need. Mark 11:24 gives a perfect example of the prayer of petition. Jesus says, "Therefore I tell you, whatever you ask in prayer, believe that you have received it, and it will be yours."

This particular prayer is also referred to as the prayer of faith because you are supposed to approach God in a faith-like manner expecting that when you pray to Him, He will answer you.

**Prayer of Agreement** - This prayer is centered on everyone involved in the prayer agreeing with each other. It is not enough to hope or assume that everyone is on the same page. There has to be a certainty that everyone is in unity regarding the need and the expected outcome.

> Again, truly I tell you that if two of you on earth agree about anything they ask for, it will be done for them by my Father in heaven (Matthew 18:19).

**Prayer of Intercession** - The word "intercessor" comes from the root word "intercede." The prayer of intercession allows for one to intercede and petition on behalf of someone else. You are going in between and intercepting. You become the advocate for the person you are praying for as if you are taking the hand of God and the hand of the one for whom you are petitioning and bringing the two together.

In Philippians 1:3-5, Paul mentions his intercession on behalf of the people of Philippi, "I thank God in all my remembrance of you, always in every prayer of mine for you all making my prayer with joy, because of your partnership in the gospel from the first until now."

**Prayer of Binding and Loosing** - The prayer of binding and loosing can be found in Matthew 18:18-19 when Jesus tells us that whatever you bind on earth will be bound in heaven, and whatever we loose on earth, will be loosed in heaven.

Jesus shows us the authority we have as believers. The authority is the jurisdiction or power to make a decision or the right to give commands. The Lord has given each of us authority, and we have to use it to carry out the work of the kingdom. The authority has been given to the believer in Christ Jesus to bind and loose. This is the key.

Binding means to fasten and tie. To forbid or prohibit. When you bind something you are forbidding it, prohibiting it from happening and putting it in chains. It is almost like a spiritual handcuff. We can't bind things out of our will, but we can bind them based on the Word. We can bind evil spirits.

Loosing means to release something that has been tied or fastened; to release and set free. It is the opposite of binding. You are untying it and setting it free. It refers to setting the captive free. If you bind something, you *must* loose something in its place or you are giving it an open space to come back and occupy. Think of it in terms of salt and pepper. When someone asks for salt, the rule is you always pass the pepper along with it, as a couple.

Once you identify that something is not the will of God, you have the authority to bind it up and loose the kingdom of God. For example: "I bind pride and I loose humility. I bind deception and loose truth."

For our prayers to be heard, we must be sure nothing is hindering them. The purpose of prayer is not to get what we want, but to learn to want what God desires to give us. However, if our wills are not surrendered, we will hold up our prayers until they are in alignment with God's agenda. We must be willing to accept the will and way of God.

Unconfessed sin in your life, which you know of and tolerate, will render your prayers powerless. Disobedience to God can hinder our prayers. That includes partial and delayed obedience. Partial obedience is still disobedience.

Pride is another hindrance to our prayers that creates a stumbling block. We lack the level of transparency needed in prayer due to fear of exposure or other reasons.

The lack of faith is also a definite hindrance to prayer. This is simply due to a trust issue with God. People are reluctant to put their full faith in God but, every day will trust people who aren't perfect and will likely disappoint them.

Unforgiveness is a major reason our prayers are unanswered. Jesus lets us know we can't expect to be forgiven if we are not willing to forgive. Forgiving and being forgiven are inseparable. When you forgive, not only is your heart made right, but it is lighter as well because you are no longer carrying that load.

Wrong motives in prayer cause you to pray "amiss." You do not receive because your heart's posture is not right. God is not going to answer your prayer for a new car, bae or to buy a house just so you can stunt on your haters. No! We have to make sure we do our due diligence so that when we pray to God, we have clean hands, pure hearts, and sound minds. Then our prayers will be heard and answered.

Once you create a prayer life, devotion time in the Word, and study the scriptures, you will see how much your life will change. The power of prayer still changes things. When you pray in the name of Jesus, everything must bow to the power and authority of His name. Anxiety bows! Cancer bows! Tumors bow! Depression bows! Divorce bows! Everything bows to that name. There is power in the name of Jesus to break chains and destroy yokes.

Your prayers will keep you sustained and hopeful while providing peace when it seems the currents are trying to overtake you. You will no longer wonder what your Father has to say because your time in prayer will reveal all things as it opens you up to a deeper understanding and revelation of

God the Father. Be committed to prayer and believe that what you pray will become what you see.

## **Spiritual Assessment**

If you find yourself struggling with prayer, get a journal or notebook that is just for your prayers and journal. Write your prayers to God. Set aside a designated time to pray each day. Use the Bible to assist you in praying Scripture while ensuring you are reading the Word daily for more effective prayers. Make sure you write the dates on your journal entries, so you can go back and read them as a resumé of the prayers God answered.

# Chapter 8
# Allow Me to Reintroduce Myself

> Therefore, if anyone is in Christ, the new creation has come: The old has gone, the new is here (2 Corinthians 5:17).

Here you are! You have made it through the autopsy results and you are still reading. That lets me know there is still some hope, which lies on the inside of you, and it should be.

I know it might not feel good having the light shine on all of the dark places in your life. However, they need to be evaluated or changed completely to assassinate all of hell's plans against you and to fulfill your God-given purpose.

The amazing thing about God is that He loves us, even when we have fallen short and drifted away. In Matthew 15:24, He says that He was sent to save the lost sheep of the house of Israel. He isn't looking for perfect people but willing people. People who are bold enough to know that they may not have it all together right now, but they are willing to give it another try.

God showed me that many people backslide for two reasons:

1. Everything they tried to accomplish was outside of the will of God
2. They tried to accomplish everything without the assistance of God

God said people may have failed you, and you may have failed yourself, but this time, He is saying, "My child, try again – but this time with me." I can hear someone saying, "But what about all of the terrible things I have done, said or thought?" or you're saying, "What are people going to say about me?"

Let me help you get free today. Romans 8:1 says, "Therefore, there is now no condemnation for those who are in Christ Jesus." In other words, the things people try to hold against you don't matter to God, and it shouldn't matter to you. God has extended His grace, mercy, and forgiveness to you, now it's your job to receive it.

Yes, you had premarital sex. Yes, you had a child out of wedlock. Yes, you were addicted to pain meds. Yes, you have failed as a parent. Yes, you made a stupid decision. Acknowledge it; repent; turn to God and start living the abundant life!

Most importantly, don't you dare beat yourself up after you have been forgiven by God. Your past does not define you. Don't self-sabotage new relationships, connections, opportunities or open doors in the name of feeling worthy or deserving based on knowing the truth about yourself. Understand and resolve in your mind that your past doesn't change what God has already said about you or His plans for you.

If anything, your past will be used as a stepping stone that will lead you into your destiny.

Instead of asking God why life's circumstances had to happen to you, change your perspective and ask God why He wanted it to happen for you. What did He want all of those trials, tribulations, and failures to teach you? Once you receive an answer from God, use it is a teaching tool in the future for yourself, others, and the generations that will come behind you.

God has too much in store for you to be bound by what you used to do or even did today. Shake off that dirt the enemy tried to bury you in. Remove those graveclothes because the power of the living God has rendered the enemy's devices for you inoperable and has declared you a grave robber who is victorious. He has come to set the captive free. Be free! And as you get free – stay free!

How do you stay free? By remaining in His presence and in His will. God has called you to be a light in this world. Matthew 5:16 tells us to let our light shine before others so they can see our good deeds and glorify God. When you allow God to shine through you, use you as a mouthpiece here on the earth to proclaim His goodness, heal the brokenhearted and help set the captive free, the enemy cannot penetrate the light, purpose or the blood of Jesus. His blood is our defense against the plots of the enemy.

As you let your light shine, darkness will automatically be driven away. Where light is, darkness cannot reside.

> The light shines in the darkness, and the darkness has not overcome it (John 1:1).

If you stay in God's presence, you will find just what you need to move forward, walk in freedom, and get out of that backslidden and dark place. Everything that has tried to kill you, God has given you the power to overcome and outlive it. Think about how many times you thought you were going to die in what you have now survived.

> Now the Lord is the Spirit, and where the Spirit of the Lord is, there is freedom (2 Corinthians 3:17).

Here are some practical tips for your transformation:

1. Set time out in your schedule to read the Word and meditate on it. You can use different Bible study methods to make your study time more productive and effective.

2. Connect yourself to like-minded believers who will help you on that journey while holding you accountable at the same time.

3. Find a church family to connect with that preaches the solid Word of God and that you

can partner with to help bless the kingdom. Attending an online church is good but community and fellowship with a local assembly is life-changing and provides additional accountability.

4. Encourage others along the way so you can show them the faithfulness of God regarding His children.

5. Discover your spiritual gifts, seek training and operate in them. God is calling you to be all He has made you to be. The world is waiting for the "new" you. It is time for you to "walk that walk" and be bold in the Lord.

Don't try to persuade people that you have changed. Just live a lifestyle of holiness and be sold out to God. Step by step. Day by day. It's a process.

Eventually, they won't be able to find you in the last place they saw you. With all of the evidence of how jacked up you were, one thing they won't be able to deny is the healing, redeeming and restoring power of God manifested in and through your life. They will see that if God can do it in your life, He can definitely do it in theirs.

When they ask what has gotten into you or why you have changed simply say, "Allow me to reintroduce myself! I am a chosen people, a royal priesthood, a holy nation, and I am God's special possession. I am forgiven, I am redeemed, set free and a manifestation of the goodness of God. I am because He is."

Learn how to fight, pray and war for your freedom. Even on a bad day, you still stand tall knowing that you are a child of God. Don't allow the devil to make you throw in the towel. If you weren't a punk in the streets, then you bet not be a punk in the kingdom.

Stand your ground, ready yourself with the armor and declare war on the enemy letting him know that he may have had your mind, family, marriage, children, career, dreams, goals, and gifts in the last season of your life, but you won't give up that quick ever again.

This is a new you with a new anointing, boldness, strength, resilience, and fight! And everything that God has promised you and those connected to you, you will have and no devil in hell can stop it!

The devil should have gotten you before you picked up this book. It's time for you to reintroduce yourself to him as the child of God that you have gotten reacquainted with.

Welcome Back! I'm thankful that you have resurrected from your spiritual death. That glow, joy, peace, smile, and freedom hits differently when you have survived the worst of times. Don't allow any doubter, naysayer or hater stop you from walking in total and complete healing.

# About the Author

Janay Roberson is an author, visionary, leader and dynamic speaker from Hickman, KY. She has a love for the word of God and an anointing to preach and teach the gospel. Her ministry is one that is marked by prophetic intercession, deliverance, healing, and revelation.

With her messages of hope and healing, she has the uncanny ability to reach people from various ages and all walks of life. She is often referred to as a "spiritual midwife" for her commitment to disciple and unlock the visions, purposes, and dreams lying dormant inside both men and women.

She is the founder of "Awaken U" Women's Ministry, a Christian-based organization designed to empower and encourage women to ignite their love for God while awakening their passion, purpose, and pursuit. Janay loves people and is committed to equipping and encouraging others to live up their fullest potential.

Being devoted to scholastic achievement, Janay is a graduate of the University of Tennessee at Chattanooga and received a master's degree from Western Kentucky University. She resides in Chattanooga, TN and serves as a Marketing Director in Higher Education.

# STAY CONNECTED

To reach Janay Roberson to share your thoughts or arrange speaking engagements, book signings, seminars, and/or workshops, please email the author at: info@janayroberson.com

**Facebook**- Janay Roberson
**Instagram**- @janayroberson
**YouTube**- Janay Roberson
**Twitter**- @janayroberson_

Visit the author's website at:
www.janayroberson.com

Made in the USA
Columbia, SC
05 September 2019